SECRET

Mama Jane's
SECRET

WALKING IN DEEP FRIENDSHIP WITH GOD

CHAD NORRIS
FOREWORD BY LEIF HETLAND

BRIDGEWAY

ISBN: 978-1-947165-35-9

BRIDGEWAY

bridgewaynetwork.org

God is calling you into the greatest friendship the world has ever known.

For additional resources, teaching, and content, please visit

MamaJanesSecret.com

dive deeper into identity, family, living a naturally supernatural lifestyle, being seated at the king's table, and more

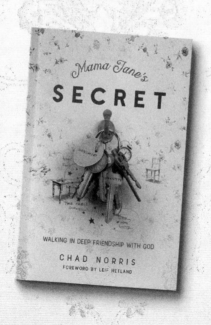

contents

dedication

Special Thanks to Dawn Sherrill Porter, Theresa Harris, and Brittney Banks. This book was a group effort and I know full well this would have never happened without all three. We are family. I love all three of you. Blake, if not for you, this book would not be what it needed to be. Thank you for your gift and hard work.

I dedicate this book to The Wolfpack. You four make me laugh every single day of my life. When it's all over and we catch the big red wagon out of here, I will look back and smile at the life that we have shared together.

Big Show: You are our fearless protector and defender. Sometimes I wish someone would try to hurt me when you are around just to see what you would do. Your heart is as big as your 6 foot 8 frame. I love you big fella.

Block: You are the most Christian person I know. Your level of humility, integrity, and honor inspire the rest of the pack. Naming you Blockhead in the third grade is one of the highest honors in my life. At some point, I do hope you will learn how to send a text. I love you.

Virgil: You threw the tightest spiral of anyone at Westview Elementary in the 3rd grade. You have been loyal to me and have been a constant true friend my entire life. You carry the DNA of your Dad and I can't wait to see him again in heaven. I love you.

Sterl: I think that if my car broke down on the side of the road 9 hours away from you that you would drive to help me. You are loyal beyond belief to this pack. Sometimes I daydream about what it would be like to see your Gamecocks win it all. This Pack could only imagine what you would do. I love you.

You four guys make me not take myself too seriously. Thank you for the literal joy that you bring to me every single day. I have never in my life laughed harder with anyone I've ever known than you idiots. We are all grown up now but not really. I want to sincerely thank each of you for how bright you make my life. I hope I live long enough to preach ya'lls funerals. As Big Jim says, "Let's keep making memories." In the end men, all we have is our relationships. And above all, Go Dawgs.

Foreword

He who has seen Me has seen the Father

John.14:9

One of my greatest desires and dreams is that these words of Jesus would be my life as well. Since my Baptism Of Love almost eighteen years ago, waves of liquid love from Papa God transformed me from an orphan living for God to a beloved son living *from* God. We have a love message to share; how we share it makes all the difference. *Mama Jane's Secret* is the recipe that all of us can follow to receive, become, and release how good God is and how loved we are.

History books may never tell you the story of a grandmother who affectionally is called "Mama Jane" by her grandchildren. History books will never tell you that Nellie Clyde Wilson, an unknown hero, had a son who ended the Cold War.

A mother with an ocean of love raised two boys in the middle of hardship, poverty, and much pain. President Ronald Reagan often said his mother was the most influential person in his life.

Mama Jane's legacy paved the way for what Chad Norris is now walking in. The secrets that Chad received from Mama Jane are perhaps the most needed messages of our time.

This book displays everything I love about Chad—his honesty, humor, humility, and his radical, practical, personal approach and devotion to God's power, love and wisdom.

If you desire to be a friend of God and make a radical difference for His kingdom, you must receive Mama Jane's secret.

The greatest compliment I can give to my friend Chad is that he has become the secret, *a true friend of God*.

Friendship with God is seen in his marriage to Wendy and as a father to his kids. His *sonship* has become *friendship* followed by a big *apostleship*. *Relationship* with the Father, Son, and Spirit has become a *family movement* of sons and daughters that will have a greater impact on the world than Ronald Reagan.

The stories from *Mama Jane's Secret* have the power to speak the truth to us in love, to transform us, to remind us that we are part of something bigger than ourselves, a kingdom family of sons and daughters who know that the impossible is possible.

Get ready to receive your upgrade!

I am honored to be considered a friend and a spiritual papa.

Much love,

Leif Hetland

Founder & President, Global Mission Awareness
www.globalmissionawareness.com
www.calledtoreignbook.com

Introduction

GROWING UP IN SPARTANBURG, South Carolina, in a very close family provided me with a foundation of love and security, a lot of which flowed from my grandmother who I affectionately called "Mama Jane." Our family made frequent trips to Mama Jane's house in the small town of Thomson, Georgia. My grandfather passed away in 1977, leaving Mama Jane to love on her grandchildren alone, which she did exceptionally well. She was one of the kindest people I have ever known. As I look back I realize that her love unintentionally showed us what the Father is like. I once heard Graham Cooke ask the question, "Who is the kindest person you have ever known? Whoever that is, imagine God being even more kind." For me the answer to this question is easy, it's Mama Jane. She was a beautiful reflection of our very kind and loving heavenly Father. In fact, she is my biggest hero. When I was younger, I heard many older people say, "Life will fly by faster than you think." Although I heard what they were saying, I never took it too seriously. Now here I am, a 45-year old man writing a book about the Kingdom of God and the traits of a great woman I once did life with. What I wouldn't give to go back and spend just one more day with her. Even now as I type this, I can recall the den in her modest home where I spent untold hours playing on the floor with my toys. It was a safe place for me and my siblings.

Throughout the years Jane played her grandparent role in raising my siblings and me, she never once talked to us about signs, wonders, and healings. I never had a conversation with her about the prophetic. I simply watched her carry traits that would one day be the lens the Father would use to help me better understand His nature. I had no inkling that one day I would lead a church that would be a bridge between the Word and Spirit, where the prophetic, healings, deliverances, and all of the gifts of the Spirit would be in operation while the Kingdom of God is taught. Part of my motivation for writing this book is to help others understand the principles and paradigms that enable us to build a deep friendship with God, and live out Kingdom relationship in your own unique God-given identity. I want to help as many people as possible to build deep friendship with the One who made us.

I've come a long way since my nervous breakdown 17 years ago. As I press into relationship with God, I consistently find Him to be all that my heart desires and so much more. I am constantly overwhelmed at how often He points me back to what I learned as a child through Mama Jane. Her great love for me and for God inspired in this beloved grandson a desire to know God as she knew him; to understand the unchanging characteristics and principals of His Kingdom. She had secrets that have taken me years to fully understand; secrets that have led me to the goodness of God. The more I explore what it means to be a deep friend of God, the more natural it becomes to operate in the gifts of His Spirit on a consistent level. I want everyone to experience a "Mama Jane" relationship with the Father. Because there is nothing on this earth that can compare to the peace of the One who created it all.

I believe God sees us, His kids, as beautifully clean as His Son Jesus. This is our inheritance. Being close friends with God is the prize. My prayer for you as you read this book is that what I learned from Mama Jane will help you no matter where you are in your journey with God. May your heart grow with a desire to know Him and the unfathomable fullness of His Kingdom.

Chapter 1

A GOD OF CHALLENGE

I HATE TO RUN. To make myself feel better about my desire not to run, I like to point out that my lineage doesn't include runners. My grandfathers and father have zero stories of running except for the few times they were chased by a dog as children. So, when I told my wife, Wendy, that I needed to do something drastic to lose some weight, and that I should probably just run a marathon, she stared at me. It was one of those awkward stares—like the one you get when you are caught going back to the dessert line at Golden Corral for the third time.

Down here in the South, where I live, there's a phrase we use—"Bless your heart." We say it to someone when we have sarcastic pity on them. When I mentioned the race, Wendy looked right at me and said, "Bless your heart, babe." A stare plus a "bless your heart" was not the response I was looking for. It didn't faze me though. I was determined to shock the world and lose a few pounds in the process. Even though it was known that I had failed at every diet or fitness trick I attempted, I knew if I kept knocking on the door, eventually my Apollo Creed would fall to the mat and I would be named champion of my own household.

Then the phone call came. My brother, James G. Norris (better known as Gabe), is one of my best friends. When I saw his name on my cell phone I had no heads-up that an offer was coming. As soon as I answered the call, Gabe said, "Do you want to run in a half marathon with me in three months?" Before I could even think, I said, "Yes." Then I hung up and pouted the rest of the day. That night before I went to bed, I Googled "How to train for a half-marathon." I read the first page I came across and thought it had to be joking. I told Wendy, "I'm going to have to run from here to Birmingham before I even get to race day." This did not sound like fun. Have you ever seen someone happy while they are running? No. Runners look like they've just been tossed out of a golf cart and are trying to catch up in order to get back in the cart. After all, God did not put humans on this earth to run. For you to really get this picture, we need to get on the same page. I'm 5-foot-9 and weigh 215 pounds. I'm thick like a walk-on nose guard for a Division III football team. I've never had one person walk up to me in my 45 years and say, "You look like a runner."

I didn't know what to do, so the next day I drove to Dick's Sporting Goods where I met a young woman who looked like she could run 10 miles without flinching. I told her I wanted to run a half marathon, and could she help me prepare for my journey through Mordor. There was an awkward 3-second pause followed by my second stare down. "Have you thought about a 5K first?" she asked. "A what?" I replied. I don't know running vernacular, but I quickly realized she thought I was out of my league. This threw me further into Rocky Balboa mode. "I'm going to run in this half marathon or die trying," I assured her. She realized I was not playing around and we began to discuss what I needed. We talked about socks, shoes, and different kinds of shirts. Then she pulled out the item that made me freeze in my tracks—shorts. I didn't know what she wanted me to do with that scrap of fabric, but I was sure it could not cover a Ritz cracker.

"Are these shorts or underwear?" I asked. She did not think that was funny. I took these neon green shorts and went into the dressing room. I worked up a full, anaerobic sweat just getting them on. My biggest regret is that I did not take a picture of myself. They were smaller than a Brazilian model's swimsuit. Later I told my friends, "I'd rather run this marathon in dress pants then wear those demonic shorts she made me try on." I charged out of that dressing room (after I changed back, of course) and said, "No." I did leave with some great socks.

I'll never forget my first training run. I had never heard of shin splints before that day. Imagine a pit bull eating both of your shins while someone cuts you in the same place with a dull spoon—that's what shin splints feel like. It's miserable. It doesn't matter if you stretch or not, they just don't go away. I prayed over my shins almost every day, and after a few weeks the pain finally left. Once I got over the shin splints, I started to get into a groove with my training. I had one simple goal for this race: don't die. I couldn't have cared less if I finished last. I just wanted to cross that finish line.

After six weeks of training, I settled in at a 12:45 pace. To some people, this is too slow to be fathomed. In my own mind, I was like Usain Bolt flying past everybody. I was booking it. At the ten-week mark, I was finally ready for race day. Athens, Georgia was the scene for the showdown.

A few thousand people showed up for the Chick-Fil-A Connect Race Series annual half marathon. There's a subculture in running that I knew nothing about until I got out of the car in Athens. Turning to my brother, I said, "I genuinely believe I am the fattest runner in this race." I was not sarcastically self-deprecating, just dead serious. I've never seen so many skinny people in my life. Happy, skinny, stretchy, and jubilant people were everywhere. They could not wait to get to the starting line. Meanwhile, I was nervous. At the starting line, there were some signs that read 7:00, 7:30, 8:00, etc. I asked my brother what they were for and he said, "Don't worry about those—you just get in the back of the line."

Bless my heart.

"YOU" ONLY BETTER

The gun went off, and 3,000 people took off like Forest Gump. My heart was pounding. A half-mile in I developed a cramp that felt like I had lead poisoning on my left side. I could barely breathe. I remember thinking, "I have 12 and a half miles left." I banged around those first two miles like a sputtering truck. That's when I saw "him." He was, to put it bluntly, a fat guy. This guy, who outweighed me by at least 50 pounds, came barreling by me like an Olympic athlete. I turned my iPod off for a second and said aloud to myself, "No." Every man has something deep down inside of him that relishes the clanging of battle and the thrill of competition. I had found the one guy out of 3,000 runners fatter than me and I was ready to take him down. I was going to beat this guy. For at least two miles I was unable to find fat guy. Yet, even though I could not see him, I thought about him constantly. I remembered what it was like to see the ocean for the first time as a child. That's what it felt like when I finally saw fat guy for the second time. Exhilarating.

Around mile 6, there was a Red Cross station to my right. It was not too far from the University of Georgia football stadium and I got caught up in the memories of going to college there. Between those memories and Coldplay playing on my iPod, I was almost in tears. At this point, I knew I had to get something to eat fast because I was losing all my energy. There was a guy at the Red Cross station who was skinnier than a vegan on a diet. He was a little too excited for my taste. He asked me, "Would you like some water?" I said, "No, I would actually like a Chipotle Burrito." Behind him was a teenage girl who said, "Would you like some pudding packs?" I had not eaten pudding since the third grade, but I grabbed two packs and scarfed them down. The vegan then said to me, "Don't drink Gatorade after eating those—it's not good for you." I just figured it wasn't good for vegans and went ahead and drank four little cups of Gatorade and took off after the fat guy. He was about 200 or 300 yards ahead of me, and I knew I was in for a battle. Desperate times call for desperate measures, so I changed over from Coldplay to Pearl Jam on my iPod. The song "Even Flow" came on as I sped up to chase my prey.

For the next four miles I felt like a racing greyhound chasing a fake fat rabbit around a track. No matter what I did, I could not catch the fat guy. At one point I said aloud to the Lord, "He is literally the fastest fat guy in America." I was begging God to slow him down, snap his hamstring, humble him in any way possible, just so I could pass him. At mile 10, I got within a hundred yards of him, but I could not catch him. At that moment, I conceded defeat and thought, "At least nobody will ever even know or care that he beat me." Then, around mile 12 the unthinkable happened. Fat Rabbit started to walk. With one mile to go, I had a chance. That next mile was like something out of a Spielberg movie. We locked eyes at one point and he knew exactly what I was doing. He stared me down and I looked him right in the eye. It was two fat guys fighting to the death—two stubborn mules chasing destiny.

With 500 yards to go to the finish line, I thought he was going to clip me. Then out of nowhere, as I heard the band playing at the finish line, I somehow put it into another gear. I caught and passed him right at the end. My brother was waiting to give me a big hug at the finish line, but I ran right past him. I crossed that finish line running like one of those big Spanish bulls in Pamplona. As I crossed the line, I looked up at the clock and could not believe what I saw—I ran the race 46 minutes faster than my training pace. It took a few seconds for this to really sink in. Chasing someone competitively had driven me to blow my training time out of the water. I knew in that moment I was capable of more than I thought. After the race, I looked for that man for a few minutes, but I never found him. I wanted to sincerely thank him for pushing me. Even though he had no idea he made me run harder, I still wanted to thank him.

Recently, I was working out at a CrossFit gym with some friends. I completed a workout called "The 12 Days of Christmas." Believe me when I say it is the hardest physical thing I have ever done in my life—even harder than that half-marathon. Toward the end of the workout, I heard the Holy Spirit say loudly, "Go harder." God was challenging me to stretch beyond my own human limits. As you walk longer with Him, do not be surprised when He starts pushing you to be someone you've never been—you, but only better than you can imagine. He is a God of challenge. To better understand that concept, let's go back to the beginning and explore what it means to live as a Kingdom family.

Chapter 2

KINGDOM FAMILY

THE CHRISTIAN LIFE ISN'T JUST ABOUT shooting up into the sky when you die. At its heart, the Christian life is about family. This idea may require a paradigm shift in your thinking. Here's an example of what I mean. I asked 25 people the question, "Who is Adam?" and 24 answered the question the exact same way. Before you read any further, think about your own answer. Once you have it, go to Luke 3:37-38. Although these may seem like odd verses to read right now, just stay with me.

the son of Methuselah, the son of Enoch,
the son of Jared, the son of Mahalalel,
the son of Kenan, the son of Enosh,
the son of Seth, the son of Adam,
the son of God.

Luke 3:37–38

Of the people I asked, 24 said that Adam was the first man ever created. Only one person said he was the first *son*. "Son" is the operative word here. Why the big deal over one word? Because that one word can lead to a life-changing breakthrough of understanding, or to a serious misconception. I believe that one of the most dangerous things in the world is a misconception. Wars are fought over misconceptions. A misconception can lead to death, even literally. The men who flew the planes into the Twin Towers fully believed they were doing the right thing. If you believe in the core of your being that junk food is healthy for you and no one can speak truth into your life, then you may suffer a fate similar to the guy in *Super Size Me* who ate McDonald's three times a day for 30 days and almost died. Just because you are passionate about something doesn't mean you are right about it. Passion can be so overrated. A misdirected passion can become a misconception, and misconceptions can lead to death. Hosea 4:6 says, "my people are destroyed from lack of knowledge." Jesus never said truth would set anyone free. He said *knowing* the truth would set us free. (See John 8:32) There's nothing wrong with saying that Adam was the first man ever created— it's actually a correct statement. However, the difference between the word "man," and the word "son" is like night and day. Satan likes to misdirect our understanding just a little bit so that we become more passionate about a doctrine than the reality of a Person.

In my opinion, as many as 95% of evangelicals in the West probably view God as a doctrine to believe rather than the One to build a relationship with. It has been my experience that very few Christians truly believe that we are literal sons and daughters of God. Granted, it's not the easiest concept to wrap our natural mind around; we need Holy Spirit inspiration for this. You see, when God created Adam, He didn't make a man, He made a son. This difference is not insignificant. We know that Adam is not the ontological son of God like Jesus Christ is, yet Paul compares the two in Romans 5 and 1 Corinthians 15. Adam came from God and bore His image. He is not just another human. He literally *came from God Almighty*. From the Scriptures, we see that God has always desired deep friendship with people. He created Adam to do more than just work in a garden. God created Adam for intimacy. They walked together in the Garden in the cool of the evening, in relationship. In Exodus 4:22, Hosea 11:1, and Jeremiah 31:9, Israel is also referred to as God's son. Even though God designated Israel to be His chosen people for all time, like Adam, they too broke covenant with Him. Being chosen by God doesn't guarantee obedience. Obedience flows out of relationship. It's about being sons and daughters, it's about being family.

God desired so much to restore broken relationship that He sent His Son Jesus Christ to redeem the curse that started when Adam committed treason. The fruit of redemption is our deep friendship with God. That's where it began and where it ends. Jesus Christ, the Son of God, lived a sinless and perfect life and then gave up His life to be resurrected so that we too might live. He conquered the death brought about by broken covenant relationship. Because of Jesus, we are now reconnected to the Father for the closest relationship possible through the blood sacrifice of our Lord for all who confess faith in Him. When we understand God's nature, it is easier to know how He will behave towards us. God is not a doctrine to figure out, He's an actual person who wants to walk with you. This is why Jesus said "our Father" so often. The second word of the Lord's prayer is "Father."

At the time Jesus taught the disciples to pray this prayer, they were struggling to figure out how He was doing signs and wonders. If we paraphrase Matthew 6:9-13 just a little, you can imagine the disciples saying, "Jesus, we've been watching you for a year. You're walking on water, blind eyes are opening and then there's the whole Lazarus thing. You're raising people from the dead! We know you pray a lot so how about you teach us how to pray like you." This little exchange between the disciples and Jesus gave us the Lord's prayer. Notice that Jesus didn't begin the Lord's Prayer with "our Leader," or "our General," "our King," or "our Majesty." He began with "our Father." He didn't say, "My Father." He said "our Father" because He is the Father of us all. Jesus has included us in His conversation with the Father. This must have been a difficult concept for the disciples to understand.

If you remember, in the Old Covenant, God was known as a very distant person, someone far removed and remote, who didn't always come off as a warm and fuzzy God. In Exodus for example, God says very matter-of-factly, "If you don't consecrate your animals I'll kill them" (Paraphrase of Exodus 19:12-13). When Jesus showed up and started calling God, "Abba," which is Aramaic for "Our Father," it's not a stretch to think that His followers were confused. Can't you just hear Simon Peter saying, "Jesus, can we just call a quick timeout? I've listened to stories passed down from generations and generations and God doesn't seem very relational to me." Or how about Nathaniel, who was a Jew. I can imagine him thinking, "You are not sounding very Jewish, Jesus. What do you mean "our Father?" And things got even crazier when Jesus ascended and Paul began teaching, "So you are no longer a slave, but God's child; and since you are his child, God has made you also an heir" (Galatians 4:7). I think the 21st century church struggles as much as the 1st century church did to understand that we are God's family. God is about intimacy.

When we step into the revelation of the intimacy that is possible between God and man, the gifts, the fruits of God's Spirit, have an opportunity to explode in our lives. I've seen this in my own life. I went from having a nervous breakdown in my late 20's to now leading conferences and workshops on helping people hear the voice of God clearly and operate in power. I know from personal experience that the breakthrough we experience can give us revelation to hear the Father in the same way Jesus was able to hear Him, and to ". . . do the works I have been doing, and they will do even greater things than these . . ." (John 14:12).

In the Garden of Eden, Elohim took some clay, dirt, and dust and whoosh—He breathed life into it creating man. When Adam opened his eyes, the first thing he saw was God looking at him with what had to be the most tender eyes imaginable. From that breathtaking beginning the two became friends. Scripture says that Adam and God walked together in the Garden in the cool of the day. Can you imagine what that was like? Then the goodness of God made woman out of Adam's rib so that he would have a helpmate. Together in intimacy and friendship, Adam and Eve were given authority to name the animals. They had something great. They had family. They had intimacy with God. It was this beautiful intimacy that enraged Satan. This fallen angel who desired to raise his throne above the stars of God, to sit enthroned on the mount of assembly, on the utmost heights of Mount Zaphon, to ascend above the tops of the clouds and make himself like the Most High (See Isaiah 14:13-14) set about to do everything he could to separate man from God. He's still at it, busy trying to steal, kill and destroy the people of God.

OUR FATHER

I think it's important that we ask the question, "Why did Jesus come to earth?" You've probably heard the standard church answer that goes something like, "Well, brother, Jesus was sent so you can go to heaven when you die." According to that answer, it's all about heaven. For a lot of people, getting to heaven is just about staying out of hell. They aren't thinking in terms of having a relationship with Jesus in heaven. For them, Jesus is simply their escape ticket out of the fiery pit. They don't understand that the Gospel is about so much more than a ticket to heaven. 1 John 3:8 says that Jesus came to destroy the works of the devil. What are the works of the devil? To separate us from God. Eternal life is not about going to a place. It is about intimacy with the Father who made us. It is about having an intimate relationship with Him *right now and in heaven when we die*. Jesus didn't come just to take you to an afterlife. He came to reconnect and re-establish your relationship with Abba Father. We can know Jesus and still live as spiritual orphans instead of sons and daughters who are a part of God's family. The orphan heart isn't pretty. Just look at the biggest orphan of all time—Satan.

Spiritual orphanhood mimics orphanhood of the natural. An orphan is a child with no mom or dad, who is being raised by someone who did not bring them into this world. If we are living like spiritual orphans, we confess that Jesus Christ was on the cross and that we will go to heaven when we die, but act as though we don't have a Father. We search for spiritual fathers and mothers and don't understand why we can't get our satisfaction and needs met through people. Jesus said, "And do not call anyone on earth 'father,' for you have one Father, and he is in heaven" (Matthew 23:9). My life changed when I went from seeing Jesus as a theology to seeing Jesus as my literal big Brother. I'm not talking metaphorically. I mean that Jesus is *literally* my big Brother.

When I comprehended the first two words of the Lord's prayer, I went from being in a fetal position dealing with intense anxiety at age 28 to seeing blind eyes open at age 29. What happened? I started to believe that God is *literally* my Father. This is why the first two words of the Lord's prayer, "Our Father," are so incredibly important. The revelation in those two words changed my life. Colossians 1:21-22 says I am as clean as Jesus, and presented before the same Father as holy. I'll never forget riding down the road and asking the Father, "You're telling me You love me as much as You love Jesus?" When I heard Him reply, "Yes," something happened to me in that moment. I got hungry and I started "eating." The hungrier I got, the more I ate. I discovered that the more you eat of His flesh and drink of His blood—the more you feast on Jesus, the manna from heaven—the easier it is to walk a life of faith. His yoke is easy and His burden is light. Once this revelation took hold in me, I actually started using the word "happy" in relation to spiritual things.

Growing up I didn't encounter a sense of happiness or joy with God. My family went to church because it's what we were supposed to do. Thankfully all that has changed for me. Now, as a pastor, I actually enjoy Monday mornings more than I do preaching on Sunday. I love just taking a walk with God. I can go to the lake and just spend time with Him, not really saying anything, just thinking about Him. My goal isn't to find material for the next sermon, or to post on social media. I just want to be with my Father. I understand why Jesus sometimes needed a boat to get away from people. He grew up in sonship and understood that life is not about performing for other people, it is about relationship with the Father. I don't say this to dishonor our earthly parents. I love my parents. Yet I know that it's possible to get to a place where our heavenly Father is more real than our earthly father. I know this sounds a little uncomfortable. You see, in the Kingdom, your earthly father is not your dad. He's actually your brother. Sounds strange doesn't it? What does that mean? It means that your earthly father is called to steward you and present you before your heavenly Father, who is the one who created you. God is actually your real Father. In fact, we're all siblings with one Dad. Jesus Christ is our big Brother, our High Priest and our King. He's the Bridge to the Father. Jesus described the Father this way, "for the Father is greater than I" (John 14:28).

Jesus came to reconnect us to our Father, to get us back to Eden, to invite us to the family feasting table. He didn't pray, "Our father, which art in heaven, hallowed be thy name. Thy kingdom go up there. And let me take all these pathetic sinners with me and just hang on until then. God, get us there. Amen." Jesus didn't pray that way, but that is how many Christians live. Jesus prayed for our Father's will to be done *on earth as it is in heaven.* He did everything He did because He had such intimate connection, such deep friendship, with the Father. Do you realize that the Father wants to be intimately connected and have a deep friendship with you, as He did with Jesus? I'm here to tell you that when you realize this truth, and live from this place of intimacy and friendship, it's going to change the way you see things. You will start to see through different lenses, a different set of glasses. These new lenses don't make you better than anyone else. They just enable you to see as your heavenly Father sees. God is calling you into the greatest friendship the world has ever known. He's willing to give you the time it takes to build a friendship, to learn to trust.

In Colossians 3:1–2, Paul tells us to, "set your hearts on things above, where Christ is, seated at the right hand of God. Set your minds on things above, not on earthly things." The heavenly realm Paul speaks of trumps the earthly realm, and requires something from us. We have to participate. We have to shift our thinking. Take Elisha for instance. One day Elisha was doing whatever he was doing. I picture him combing his beard. A servant came in and said, "We're going to die," and Elisha responded, "O sovereign Lord, open up his eyes." What eyes was Elisha talking about? The servant's eyes were open in the natural. He could see armies coming down on them, but he didn't have the spiritual eyes to see what God was going to do. Elisha, however, was seeing with spiritual eyes. He saw the divine protection that was on the way so he prayed for the servant's eyes to be opened in the same way. When the servant went back outside, he saw the divine protection all around them. (See 2 Kings 6:15-18) Surely God didn't grow new eyeballs on the top of this guy's head. In answer to Elisha's prayer, the servant's spiritual eyes were opened. When Jesus says, "Let him who has eyes, let him see," He's not talking about our empirical knowledge. It's about more than what we see or hear physically. Until we get beyond our five senses, we can be in Christ but live as orphans all the days of our lives. The moment I learned to see things the way He sees them, everything changed. This same "sight" is available to you, in relationship with Him. Your life can change in one moment with one change in the way you see. I want *His* eyeballs, literally. I want to see from *His* perspective. I want to hear Him, to walk with Him every moment of my life. I want Him to correct me when I fall back to a place of seeing things through natural eyes instead of seeing through His eyes of love. He *is* love and I want to see others as He sees them.

LIVING AS SONS AND DAUGHTERS

It is when we are so connected to Him, seeing through His eyes that we make the journey from spiritual orphans to spiritual sons. I wish I could make this more complicated, but it's not. Right now, the truth is no matter what you've been through in your past, in your Father's eyes, you are His literal child. He does not love the King of Glory more than He loves you. He doesn't love Adam and Eve more than He loves you. You are His family. Adam, the first son in this big family, made a tremendous mistake. Yet the Father is so good that even before He created man, He already had a plan for Jesus to come and reconcile the whole situation. He sent His Son so that whoever believes in Him shall not perish but have eternal life. (See John 3:16) What is eternal life? It is deep intimate connection, deep friendship with your Father, and it starts *now*, not in the sweet by-and-by. There is something inside of every one of you reading this book that longs for your Daddy. We attempt so many things just trying to get the attention of our Dad, and we do it in the spiritual much like we do in the natural. Here's an example from my family. I was hitting golf balls with my sons one day, and every time Jack, my 8-year-old, prepared to hit the ball he would wait to see if I was looking. He always does that. Before he hits, he looks and I say, "I see you," yet he never stops saying, "Dad, watch *this* one." Our relationship with God is no different. We can be 100 years old and still asking, "Daddy, are you proud of me?" There's something inside of us that yearns for the affirmation of our heavenly Father. Many who live as spiritual orphans were actually never loved by their earthly father. This makes the whole concept of Kingdom family harder to believe, but believe it we can because it is the truth, and His truth sets us free. (See John 8:32)

We literally have a Father who is *the* majestic Creator of everything ever created. If that's not mind-blowing enough, think on this—He makes Himself small enough to relate to you as though it's just you and Him. I don't know how He does it. The moon and stars are His footstool; He knows the whole world in detail. *All* His sons and daughters are the apple of His eye, and yet He is completely focused on you as though you are His only son or daughter. How incredible is that? And guess what? You can make the choice to let this deep friendship, this incredible sonship, dominate your life. You can wake up in the morning and embrace the truth that He loves you as much as He loves Jesus Christ; that you are protected, that there is favor on you, that not even disease can separate you from His love. The truth is that every devil in hell can come at you and it doesn't really matter because He holds you in the palm of His hand. On a daily basis, Father God invites you to the Family Table where you can feast in the presence of your enemies. Slander doesn't matter, gossip doesn't matter, your past doesn't matter when you take your place at the Table. This is too good to be true and yet it is true. The Greek word for "too good" is *euaggelion*, which means gospel. The Gospel is too good to be true, yet it's still true. I don't know about you, but I want the DNA of heaven to reside in me. I want to believe it in my gut. I don't want to limit myself or God by making the decision not to see through His eyes or love with His heart. I want to live "on earth as it is in heaven," by faith.

THIS THING CALLED FAITH

Many of us struggle to understand this thing we call faith. Just what is faith, or what is it not? Faith is not ignoring the natural realm. Faith is not denial. Faith is simply saying "Yes, the natural I'm living in is real, but there's a reality that trumps this." Jesus constantly preached the reality of the Kingdom of God. He put this reality front and center in the Lord's prayer: "Our Father which art in heaven, hallowed be thy name, thy kingdom come . . . ." He actually brought the kingdom to earth with Him, announcing its arrival. (See Mark 1:15) We are literally living in the Kingdom of God. This Kingdom exists all around us, but until you have eyes to see, you will never walk in it. To walk in God's Kingdom means to focus on Truth—to focus on Jesus. He's the answer to everything.

We should be living in the reality of such a level of deep friendship with God that we are triggering orphans all around us with a desire to know Him. There should be such a level of sonship in you that spiritual orphans don't like it. I am not talking about arrogance. When Jesus gets in you, it's actually a very humbling thing. I didn't do anything to deserve being in God's family, but you can be sure I am going to enjoy it. I'm not going to walk around like I don't have any hope. I am going to live as a son who is intimately connected with the Father; a son who is invited to dine at the family feasting table. I'm going to live as a son who knows that my heavenly Father loves me *and* likes me. I don't have to fall apart like a three-dollar bill. I'm actually destined to reign with Him. I am a loaded weapon in His Kingdom. This is personal for each of us. We're not to live like orphans, running faster and harder trying to get to the Father. I want to acknowledge that I have already made it to the Father. If I chase Him, it is to get stronger, not to prove something. Sons grow stronger, orphans continue to seek a place to belong. You belong, not because of you, but because God wants you. You can have intimacy and deep friendship with Him because Jesus has made it possible for you to be part of His literal family.

I pray that we can all get to the place where we can say, "I am just on this earth to grow in revelation of who I am in God's family and to love others." If the Father created Adam to bless him, then I ought to be blessing people wherever I go. God's aroma ought to be on me. When I know who I am, it's easier to love others. When true sons and daughters are around orphans, they bring them life. People tell me all the time, "Chad, you're funny, you're always laughing." I'm this way because I'm genuinely happy. I've done the depression thing. I've been there and I absolutely don't want to do that anymore. I have found my Father. His number one Son is my big Brother. The Holy Spirit lives in me, and angels are always around me. I am invited to feast at our Father's family Table and I like it. Why would I ever want to live any other way? Why would you? This is not denial, it is faith. We *all* get to run. We *all* get to take our place at the Table. We *all* get to live a life of intimacy. We *all* have the opportunity. Sonship is available when we embrace Him.

Chapter 3

THE FATHER'S HEART

I T HAS BEEN 15 YEARS since i received the baptism of the holy spirit. I have seen things straight out of the book of Acts—healings, miracles, signs and wonders. Yet, here I am now 15 years into walking in the Kingdom admitting that the only thing that truly matters to me is deep friendship with Father, Jesus, and Holy Spirit. This realization came into sharp focus for me after the death of a dear friend. It jarred me in a good way even though his passing took me by surprise. Having a good friend who is now standing in the presence of the God he so loves made my journey of faith so much more real. I was reminded afresh that our time here on earth is short. My friend's death put a new urgency inside of me to deeply hunger for the Father. I left the funeral by myself and became quite emotional. From the bottom of my gut I cried out, "Father, I just want to know you. I want deep friendship with you." In the weeks that followed, I began to ask myself some serious questions and to think deeply about what really matters in life. Since then, I have found that I have a clarity of thought that is bringing into focus why I am on this earth. The Father's heart is showing me that I am here to build deep friendship with Him, and to bring as many others as possible into deep relationship with Him.

TO KNOW HIM

One day, I was in my office praying over a pastor from another church. We had been talking about some of the things that God was doing with us and our churches. At one point I shared the impact my friend's death had on my life; how it had brought me to this sold out and radical place where the "one thing" for me was deep friendship with God. I told him about the clarity of thought that I was experiencing; how it supersedes even the prophetic, healing, leadership, and influence for me. I remember saying, "I'm not here to pastor a church. I'm here to know the Father." I then began to prophesy about some of the things that I was seeing over our city, Greenville, S.C., and what the Father was telling me He wanted to do here. As I prophesied, blue angelic feathers began to fall from my office ceiling. Both of us saw them with our natural eyes. Now mind you, I have never pursued signs or wonders. I've never had a desire to go after "out of the box" things like gold dust or feathers. When I was praying with this pastor and prophesying, I didn't ask the Father to make blue feathers manifest. I was simply prophesying about the importance of deep friendship with God, and what I saw coming to this city, when the feathers started to fall.

Perhaps God manifested His presence with the feathers that day in my office because I was putting a pure desire to know Him before anything else. I wasn't seeking signs and wonders. I was seeking Him. When we put "out of the box" things ahead of relationship, we get out of alignment. Cornelius did not ask to see the angel in Acts 10. He was not even Jewish. Cornelius was simply going after God with all of his heart when the angel manifested. When we critique and disregard "out of the box" encounters with God, we end up pursuing a theology over a relationship with the Father. The common thread between biblical characters who sought hard after God is that many times they had experiences that made very little sense in the natural. When you go after God with all your heart, desiring above all else to be in deep relationship with Him, don't be surprised when you begin to experience supernatural things in your life. It has happened to me.

One Sunday morning at our church, I was in the middle of a musical worship set and I said, "Father, I just want to thank you for how good you are to me." As I said those words, I immediately doubled over and began to weep. God opened my eyes to heaven for four straight minutes. When I say weep, you need to know that I am not a weeper. I'm a very laid back guy who laughs a lot. I am not one who is given over to a wide swing of emotions, especially weeping. That morning I cried so hard that two people asked me if I was ok. I cried so hard that I was having a hard time breathing. Then God gave me a vision. In the vision, there were people as far as I could see. I saw a crystal river leading up to a large city. People were on both sides of the river singing a song of worship in unison. Many of them were waving flags and banners. When I say many, I mean thousands upon thousands. To my left was an angel, standing beside me, and he did not look human. He was blue and he had a very serious look on his face. I knew he was very important. I saw all of this with my eyes open. It was like watching a movie even though I was in a worship service. This vision was so real that it completely overwhelmed me. I never expected Him to show me heaven like He did. In the middle of the vision, God said to me, "Chad, this is to prime the pump for what you will experience in your life." All of this happened when I said, "Father, I want to thank you."

I recall another Sunday when a huge glory cloud manifested in the sanctuary. It was not long after I took the job as lead pastor at Bridgeway Church. We were in worship when a huge cloud, about 70 feet in size manifested in the sanctuary. People all over the room saw it. I didn't know quite what to do so I asked God. "Father," I said, "What do you want me to do?" I had an impression to go on stage and say, "Folks, I'm not sure what to say about this cloud other than if we will keep our focus on the God of this cloud and not the cloud itself, we will have a healthy church here at Bridgeway. If we ever make signs and wonders our focus, we will lose big. If we keep our eyes on God and how to build deep friendship with Him, we will win." I then prayed to the Father and told Him that He is the One we want to know.

In Ephesians 1:17-19 Paul says, "I keep asking that the God of our Lord Jesus Christ, the glorious Father, may give you the Spirit of wisdom and revelation, so that you may know him better. I pray that the eyes of your heart may be enlightened in order that you may know the hope to which he has called you, the riches of his glorious inheritance in his holy people, and his incomparably great power for us who believe." I personally don't believe most of us have faith problems. I believe most of us have love problems. I learned a while back that faith works by love. (See Galatians 5:6) When we realize that power and gifts such as the prophetic flow from deep friendship with Him, encountering Him becomes effortless. Nothing can compare to knowing Him.

RECEIVING OUR INHERITANCE

Once you taste intimacy with the Father, nothing else satisfies. A journey into the supernatural is not a journey into signs and wonders. It is a journey into the heart of the Father of Lights. (See James 1:17) When you begin to understand who the Father is and how He sees you, you will begin to understand the reality of the life of a son, which includes manifestations of the supernatural things of God. You will understand

His ways and the naturally supernatural lifestyle He has for you. The Father is Supernatural, and intimacy with Him makes us look more and more like the reality of who He is. I love talking about the Kingdom and the responsibility that we carry as God's ambassadors. Yet, what I love more is talking about who we are as His kids. I love Jesus. I give my life to Him every day, but there is One He called "greater than I." (See John 14:28) That is the One my heart's obsession points toward. I think about Him all of the time. I want to know the Father more. I believe we see healings because the more we get to know the Father, the more we understand how much He values healing. Healing was His idea in the first place. I long to see believers who stop playing it safe, who jump in the River out of relationship. When you're in relationship with God, the supernatural is no longer weird and frightening. If you think about it, it's weird to call ourselves disciples and not see what God's disciples can see.

I believe things are changing for the Church. God has given us authority. We are capable of so much more than we think. The message of the Father's heart is no longer a conversation for one particular denomination. I believe we will see the message of the Father's heart on full display in every denomination in the coming years. Heaven is busy right now knocking down walls and ushering in the river of God's healing and deliverance in circles that have rarely if ever seen activity like this before. I am hungry for the Word. I want Him to continually wash me in the Truth of His Word. I want to walk with Holy Spirit, as a son who sees what Jesus saw. I want to see the family receive all the benefits and the inheritance we are entitled to. It is foolishness to have an inheritance and not tap into it. I want to be right in the middle of this River of the Father's love. And, I want to see you there too. Getting to the River often takes time and patience and not a little wisdom, yet the journey is so worth the effort.

LOW AND SLOW

I've resigned to the fact that I am a man of extremes. Once, in seminary, I decided that I was going to start exercising by paddling a canoe down the river to burn some calories. Small problem was that I did not have a canoe or a vehicle to tote a canoe. After some doing, I managed to find a canoe. That was when my wife decided to help me understand that the whole canoe thing was not a good idea for me for lots of reasons; reasons that only wives see. My canoe dream never became a reality. I was left to stick to power walking a few times a year.

In another season in my life, I decided that I was going to become a cook. I found this passion in the middle of a 21-day fast. The Father said to me one day, "I want you to go on a fast." This was at 9 o'clock in the morning. I replied, "Father, please confirm this 21 times over the next few hours." I immediately knew He was not kidding. You see, I have loved food from my first meal on the earth. I'm the guy that plans my next meal while I am in the middle of eating my current meal. I dream of food while I am awake and while I am asleep. I actually once dreamed that a cheeseburger saved me from a bad guy in a dream. When I told my wife that I was a foodie, she explained to me that foodies love to cook food you can't pronounce, and that I was actually not a foodie but simply a man that loves to eat food. So when the Father told me to go on a fast, I was quite shocked at the realization that I was about to embark on an inner struggle of a lifetime for me.

My first day of the fast I thought I was going to pass away and enter glory. In the middle of that first afternoon I made a decision to go to Barnes and Noble and buy a cookbook. At that time I had never purchased a cookbook in my life that I could remember. I bought this cookbook and headed back to work. I sat in my office and did something that to this day I am actually surprised I did. I opened up to the Cajun section of recipes and licked the page that had a picture of gumbo. This was my first experience with gumbo and little did I know that years later this tasty dish would become one of my best friends. Over the years, gumbo has gotten me through some rough times.

Some people search the internet for hours daydreaming about their dream homes, places to vacation, cars to buy, or music to listen to. Not me. I love to search the internet for different variations of gumbo. A couple of years after the 21-day fast ended, I decided to take the plunge and cook my own version of gumbo. I was so excited when I found a lady on YouTube teaching how to make gumbo. It was a 25 minute video, and if I watched that video once, I watched it 50 times. Then I headed out to get the Cajun trifecta of celery, onion, and green pepper which went on to become cherished friends in my kitchen in the years to come. I can barely watch football now without cutting up my three little buddies and tossing them into my homemade roux. Roux. Just saying the word makes me emotional.

Anyone interested in cooking a Cajun dish must become acquainted with the delicate concoction of roux. Roux is more complicated than a Rubik's Cube. It's two ingredients that are very difficult to navigate and takes tons of patience and understanding to master. I think God teaches us about marriage by inventing things like roux. Roux is flour and canola oil mixed together over low heat and stirred for 4 months. Actually, I may be exaggerating slightly. It does not take quite that long to make good roux, but it sure seems like it does. After slowly—and I mean slowly stirring these two ingredients together over a medium-low heat, the roux is ready in about an hour. You can't cook it too fast. If you rush roux it will taste awful. After I make my roux, I add my three little buddies and that's when the culinary magic begins in earnest. When the trifecta is cooked, I put the roux in a boiling pot of chicken broth and our house begins to smell like the 3rd Heaven. I have told the Father many times that when I come home, I would love a huge pot of gumbo waiting for me in my heavenly mansion. The smell of gumbo while football is on TV does something to me and my family that is a biblical shalom. It is a form of torture to smell my roux for the next four hours before the shrimp, sausage, chicken, scallops, and rice are finished. Gumbo is delicate and takes a long time. I've said often to my kids, "Good gumbo is low and slow friends."

Low and slow is not something that many of us are comfortable with. We tend to expect and want friendship with God to be overnight. We are tempted to jump from conference to conference looking for something from God instead of asking those people who are being used mightily by God how they developed a deep friendship with Him. The best wine to drink is the wine that has been sitting on a shelf for a very long time. Friendship with God looks no different. Many people want the influence of King David but do not want to spend the amount of time that David spent building intimacy with God. For over a decade David was running for his life from Saul. During this time, when it looked like his life was falling apart, God was doing something deep in David. We tend to want the relationship that Joseph had with God, yet few of us want to spend that much time in our own dungeon getting to know God. Simply put, deep friendship with God takes time, lots of time. To experience the "gumbo of God" you must first learn how to make the roux.

FROM MISCONCEPTION TO REVELATION

At 28 years old, I was in the single worst moment of my life, curled up in a fetal position on my kitchen floor. I was coming off of medications for clinical depression, and it was killing me. I could hear my wife in the other room talking to my brother, asking him what to do. I was out of hope and Wendy was out of hope. There comes a moment where you wonder if God is even real at all, much less if He wants to bless you. This was my moment. The seminary degree that hung on my wall meant nothing to me as I lay there on the floor crying my eyes out. I was having a nervous breakdown, detoxing from powerful chemicals from medicine. I had been trying to make sense of why I was having so many demonic dreams at night, while also suffering from pure exhaustion. I did not want to live and I did not want to die. The only word I can use to describe that season of my life was *hell*. I was going through *hell*.

Lying prone on the floor, I thought, "I just can't do this anymore." I seriously thought I was about to lose my marriage, my mind, my job. And, for the first time in my life I thought I was going to lose my faith too. I had zero belief that I would ever get through the hell I was experiencing. I later read how Henri Nouwen classified these times as the "dark night of the soul." Unless you have been there, it is difficult to understand. In these dark nights, you doubt the very existence of God Himself. You go to places you aren't sure you can survive. I felt like Jacob must have felt toward the end of his wrestling match with God. Even more, I felt like Job when he cursed even the day he was born. (See Job 3:1) The same person who had gotten me through so much on this earth in my past now seemed non-existent. I was at the end of myself. I did not know what to do.

During this season, I still had to preach to make a living. I didn't want to preach to please God, or even to help people. If anyone listening knew what was in my heart, they would have walked out of the building. I even preached through the book of Job with a team at a Bible Study, but that made my hell more real because I was focused on how this man in Scripture questioned his very existence. There's a saying that your biggest breakthroughs are preceded by your biggest breakdowns. This was certainly my biggest breakdown. One night, as I lay there trying not to sleep, I began to pray quietly. "God," I said, "If You even care or if You are even there, help. I give up." This prayer wasn't coming from someone who had not seen God as real. I had seen God do many things before. It was just that in the middle of my hell, my wrestling match, I did not care about the past. I doubted what I had seen. I doubted who He was. I doubted everything.

A week later, I traveled to Georgia to preach. While I was there, I met a young lady named Julie. Her dad was a counselor who specialized in spiritual warfare. I decided to give that type of counseling a go. Little did I know that this would be the launching pad of my new life with God.

When Wendy and I arrived at the counselor's office, I didn't know what to expect. The counselor was calm, cordial and incredibly wise. A couple of hours into our session, he prayed for me. That's when it happened. Jesus appeared to me, Chad Norris, a born and bred Southern Baptist, in a literal open vision. He walked right up to me and said, "I'm your healer. Trust me." He said it twice. Love flowed through me like liquid as I stared right at Jesus. I don't know what heaven is going to be like, but if it's anything like my experience with the King of the universe, I can't wait. The One who created it all held me. The One who walked on this earth with His disciples and flipped the world upside down was with me. I'm still not over it all of these years later. I pray I never get over it.

Wendy knew something had happened to me. I knew in that moment that I had a major problem on my hands—because the God I went to seminary to learn about was not the same God I met that day. It's hard to explain. That one encounter created a hunger in me that has not decreased to this day 15 years later. I knew enough theologically to understand that the Son and the Father were the same, (See Hebrews 1:3) and in that moment, I knew I had been tricked by the enemy. The misconception was revealed—the Father had to be just as loving as the Savior I had just experienced. Satan was unmasked.

When Wendy and I left the counselor's office, I made a plea to God. It went like this: "I'm begging You to show me who You are. I'll follow You no matter what. I don't care what happens to my life. I must know You even if it costs me everything." Starting the night, when I prayed that prayer, my misconceptions started to transform into correct conceptions of who God is, what His nature is, and how He sees me. The revelation that Our Father loves us and wants to bless us, that He wants us to have a close relationship with Him and to walk in truth, became real to me, and has remained real to me ever since. I know that I belong, that I have a home with the Father. It's so important to know that we belong. This knowing, this belonging is part of our true identity.

Chapter 4

IDENTITY

OVER THE COURSE OF MY LIFETIME I have learned so many things about myself, some of which have not been a lot of fun to process with the Holy Spirit. When I was five years old, I had an encounter with God shortly after the death of my grandfather. I was sitting outside on a rock when I heard an audible voice say, "I am going to do great things with your life for my Kingdom." At the tender age of 5 I had not formally given my life to Jesus Christ for salvation, yet I knew who it was that was talking to me. For whatever reason, I decided not to tell anyone about that experience. I simply kept it to myself. Even now when I think about it, I can remember the scene like it was yesterday.

That encounter was in 1977. The next time I would have an encounter like that was in 1994. I was in Jefferson City, Tennessee, working at a Christian Sports Camp. Late one night while sitting outside by myself in the middle of a ball field, I looked up to heaven and said, "What is it that you want from me God?" I immediately heard His audible voice answer me. He told me what He was going to do with my life. Twice in less than twenty years God gave me a glimpse of my destiny. Both times it was like hearing a message from a friend. It did not even take any faith for me to believe those two different encounters. My hair did not stand up on my neck, I did not see any angels, and neither encounter gave me goosebumps. Truth be told, most of my encounters with God are very simple and matter-of-fact.

You would think that two encounters like this would leave me few doubts about what it is that God wanted to do with my life. The truth is quite the opposite. It is easier for me to prophetically perceive what God sees in other people than to receive what He sees in me. For example, God gave me a word of knowledge about a friend of mine and his sister that was so accurate that it startled both of us. God told me my friend's sister's name and some other very specific things about her. I heard it so clearly that it did not really feel like I was exercising faith. This has happened so often over the last few years that I've lost count of the number of times God has blessed me and others with so many accurate words of knowledge. (See 1 Corinthians 12:8) With this kind of ability to hear God for other people, growing in my own identity should be simple. Yet, when it comes to my own perception of how the Father sees me as a leader, I get some kind of spiritual brain freeze. The person that has helped me the most to get over this hurdle is King David.

King David was an amazing man in so many ways. To study his life is to peel back layers. I stumbled upon a very strange verse in 1 Chronicles 14:2 (KJV) which says, "And David perceived that the LORD had confirmed him king over Israel, for his kingdom was lifted up on high, because of his people Israel." This struck me as odd because King David sure did seem to wait a long time before perceiving that he had been established as King over Israel. I mean a long, long time. Did he have a short memory of the many encounters he had already had with God to confirm this? Why did it take so long for David to perceive who God had declared him to be? I mean, Samuel poured oil on David's head, David defeated Goliath, he had success with Judah and yet he still didn't understand who God was calling him to be. Welcome to the journey of most, if not all of the people in the Kingdom of God.

As I pondered the life and times of King David, Holy Spirit led me to a book written by Dale Mast titled, *And David Perceived that He was King*. Through this book God helped me to identify my strengths and weaknesses regarding operating in the prophetic. I could "see" easily for others, but not for myself. Then came the breakthrough dream about an avocado.

I've had some strange dreams over the years, but the one I am about to describe is at the top of the food chain of strange dreams. Let me set the context before I go into the dream. In 2017 I was privileged to be part of a television show titled "Adventures with God." The filming involved Shawn Bolz and some other well-known ministers in Orlando, Florida. Darren Wilson and WP Films brought us in to film for a week about the prophetic and some hot topics in the Kingdom. A month before I went to do the filming, I was in my bedroom and I said casually to God, "I sure wish I could hear you like Shawn does." Shawn is the author of *Translating God* and *God Secrets*. He is prolific in the prophetic and uses his gift to train up hundreds of thousands of people all over the world. When I said that to God, I stopped in my tracks because for the first time in my life, I felt a literal sadness come over me from Him. I immediately knew in my spirit something was wrong. I sat down on the side of the bed and said, "Father, I don't know what's going on but I feel like you are literally upset with what I just said to you." Over the next few

moments, a stream of consciousness flooded me in my spirit, and this is
what He said to me:

> *Chad, you think that it's humility to say what you just said to me,
> but it's not. You actually are self-deprecating and not being honest
> with the gift in which you operate. You see other people through my
> lens, yet when it comes to seeing yourself, you have confused humility
> with false humility and self-deprecation. You will limit yourself the
> rest of your life until you start seeing yourself the way in which I see
> you. You see yourself as righteous because of the blood of Jesus, but
> when it comes to who you are in my Kingdom, it's easier for you to
> look down upon your gift. The enemy has convinced you that this is
> humility. It saddens me, Chad, to hear you ask me for something as
> though you don't walk in friendship with me and have the ability
> to hear me every day. Until you remove this root, you will never
> fully experience what I want from you in the prophetic.*

I was startled. It had been quite a while since I had been called out by
the Father. Even though His words did not bring condemnation, they
did bring a sharp conviction. I had been confusing humility with self-
deprecation. I'm not so sure that false humility is not the worst form of
pride. That night I went to bed and dreamed that I was laying on my
back and a doctor peeled half of my face back with a surgical instrument.
With half of my face peeled back, the doctor then pulled a full-grown
avocado seed from under my left eye. In the dream I asked, "Am I going
to die?" I never saw the doctor's face and he never answered my question.
When the avocado seed was removed, I glanced to my left and saw one
of my best friends sitting beside me. His name is Jonathan Helms and
he serves on staff with me at Bridgeway Church. We have been friends
for over twenty years. We went to Seminary together. Jonathan reached
over and helped the doctor put my face back together and all of a sudden
I sat up, looked in the mirror and it looked like the surgery had never
even happened.

When I woke up from that dream, God began to immediately download what the dream meant for me. He showed me that He was going to help do surgery on my ability to see and perceive correctly. I was going to start seeing and hearing how He perceives and sees me as a leader. He told me that He had to remove a seed of doubt, and that He was going to use my friend to help me understand that God loves me and wants me to perceive myself the way He does. I want what I'm going to say next to be so easy for you to understand that you will have to hire someone to help you misunderstand it. Ready? Until I get a proper perception of who I am in Christ, and who I am as a leader, I will greatly limit what God can do with and through me.

If you read David's story long enough, you can see his progression from knowing very little of his identity, to knowing who he was in God's eyes, to a massive amount of security in his God-given identity. David was even able to help Mephibosheth, one of Jonathan's sons, make the journey for himself. So often we are looking to someone else to impart a gift such as the prophetic to us while failing to realize that this type of growth comes most fully when we are in relationship with the Father. It can begin with a simple prayer such as, "Father, I am asking you to help me perceive how you see me." Simple but profound. What we think is humility can actually be spiritual orphanhood.

It gives me great comfort to know that King David struggled with identity issues. Let's go back and look at David's life more closely in order to understand this more fully.

AN INVITATION TO THE KING'S TABLE

God never wanted Israel to have a king. He set up a leadership structure and put judges and prophets in charge, but the Israelites looked around and saw that other nations had a king, so they started asking for a king. Then they pushed and pushed. Sometimes, when you push God hard enough and long enough, He'll give you what you don't need. As a pastor, I can't tell you how many times I have seen people take their lives and destinies into their own hands only to find out that it is never wise to make plans and then ask God to bless those plans. The wiser statement is, "Father, show me what you want me to do and I'll be just fine with that." The Israelites kept pushing and God said, "Okay. This is not going to go well, but I'm making Saul your king."

When God predicts something, He has a remarkable track record of being right. So it was with Saul, Israel's first king. To make a very long story short, Saul ended up being a very ungodly king. As a result, God anointed David to become the next king. David was probably 12 years old when Samuel first anointed him as king. Then he went back to what he was doing. It was not his time. Saul was insanely jealous and tried, for a long time, to kill David. This proved difficult in part because Saul's son, Jonathan, was David's best friend. Jonathan saved David from Saul more than once. David promised Jonathan he would take care of his family should Jonathan die before him. Jonathan and Saul were both killed in battle and David became king of Judah when he was 30 years old.

Now picture in your mind King David, enjoying feasts at the king's table, thriving in leadership. Israel had 40 years of peace and prosperity, and it was amazing. Perhaps David was telling stories of the old days and reminiscing about his friend Jonathan when he suddenly remembered his promise to Jonathan—that his family would be well taken care of. And they were, except for Jonathan's son Mephibosheth, who was lame in both feet. Mephibosheth lived in Lo-debar, the land of barrenness. David knew he must keep his promise even though Mephibosheth didn't even know the promise existed. An invitation went out from the palace to Mephibosheth, inviting him to come and sit at the King's table. I'm guessing he was surprised. Being invited to the king's table meant he would be taken care of until the day he died, or until the king was overthrown. He would be treated like a son. All of this actually happened to Mephibosheth. King David also restored to him the land that was his inheritance, and gave him overseers to work the land on his behalf. That's a pretty good deal.

So, was Mephibosheth overjoyed by this amazing turn of events? Not so much. He reacted by saying "What is your servant, that you should notice a dead dog like me?" (2 Samuel 9:8b). If we pay attention long enough to our own words, and the words of friends around us, we tend to give signs of our own orphanhood with our words. Out of the mouth, the heart speaks. (See Luke 6:45) Mephibosheth had known what it was like to be fatherless, to be without, to rely on others. This is all he knew. He knew how to fight to exist. He knew how to fight to belong. Instead of focusing on the goodness of the King, Mephibosheth focused on the fact that he was crippled, and on his own sense of unworthiness.

I believe with my entire heart that Satan's number one tactic is condemnation. Martin Luther called Romans 8, "The Gateway to the Bible." I find it interesting that the first verse of Romans 8 is, "Therefore, there is now no condemnation for those who are in Christ Jesus." Not much has changed since the days of Mephibosheth. It seems the biggest battle we go through is our own sense of unworthiness. I started walking in the prophetic 15 years ago and I have found that self-condemnation is the number one reason people have a hard time stepping into the reality of 1 Corinthians 14:1. It's practically impossible to walk in a high level of the prophetic or any other gift and at the same time develop a critical spirit towards yourself.

Picture what it must have been like for Mephibosheth. His grandfather was the first King of Israel, and his dad was the best friend of the current king. Yet, he was living without any of those benefits. He did not know what it was like to be invited into a family. He was uncomfortable at the king's table and wanted to return to Lo-debar, the land of barrenness, the place where he felt more comfortable. He wanted to return to the familiar. In those biblical days, his physical ailment was looked upon as a sign of weakness and worthlessness. He had been groomed to see himself as the opposite of the opportunity that awaited him. His thinking was essentially "old covenant" thinking. Under the Old Covenant, the connection between God and man was tenuous at best.

BACK TO EDEN

Go with me now, in your mind, to the Upper Room. Jesus and His disciples are gathered there to share what became known as the Last Supper. Jesus told His disciples He was going to institute a New Covenant, but they couldn't understand what he was saying. The Old Covenant between God and Moses had stood for thousands of years. Jesus was about to put a face on God, to show us the character of His Father. He came to reconnect us to the Father, to invite us to the King's table. He was about to make a way so that we can have deep friendship with our Father in a relationship where we will be taken care of, where angels minister to us and protect us. He was opening the door for us to go back to a place of intimacy with the Father, who is Provider and Protector. Jesus was giving us back our inheritance.

Just as Mephibosheth was brought to the king's table because of the promise made by David to Jonathan, so are we invited to the King's Table because of the promise of the New Covenant that comes through Jesus Christ. That's good news. In fact, that's awesome news. Just like Mephibosheth, we can eat at the King's Table all our days. We can enjoy the benefits of being a son. We can enjoy His kindness. For me, these are not just hyper spiritual words that are full of passion with no substance. I remember what it was like to be in a fetal position in my kitchen at age 28, with zero ability to ever believe that I would one day become good friends with the God that I was convinced was always upset with me.

The narrative of the Bible is actually an invitation back into Eden. It's an invitation back into close and intimate friendship with God. People who are looking to walk in a high level of power in the Kingdom, where healing and miracles are not just things to be studied in the Bible, are people who must settle on this conversation deeply inside of their own hearts. Friendship with God comes with great benefits. Healing and the prophetic flow out of a deep and intimate connection with Him. I have noticed over the years that all of my power encounters in the Kingdom—when I have seen people delivered of demons, healed and given shockingly accurate words of knowledge— have come from my revelation that I'm in Eden with the Father. He loves me as much as He loves Jesus Christ. This is the baseline for friendship with God. This is the baseline for a powerful life in the prophetic, where the ability to hear His voice is not predicated by me having to go to someone else to receive. We need to be raising up the next generation as men and women, sons and daughters who are getting words directly from Abba. He's our Father according to Jesus. When we settle this idea of Eden in our mind, it's the launching pad for explosive growth in our ability to hear Him for ourselves.

LEARNING TO RECEIVE BLESSING

I'd love to tell you that this revelation of Kingdom sonship happened seamlessly for Mephibosheth, that he pulled himself up to the king's table, said a heartfelt "thank you" and feasted happily ever after. That's not what happened though. Instead, when Mephibosheth came to the table, it seemed he was more comfortable in Lo-debar. If we're honest, many of us are like Mephibosheth. Very few people are comfortable receiving blessing. I truly believe that the highest form of pride is the inability to receive. We tend to think that we don't deserve intimacy or protection. Instead of focusing on the goodness of the King, Mephibosheth focused on his own inadequacies, unworthiness, and handicaps. Spiritual orphans are like Mephibosheth. They focus on their own handicaps and unworthiness instead of the provision of their King.

Spiritual orphanhood is being more comfortable in Lo-debar, the land of barrenness, than at the King's Table.

Let's get very practical here. Do you fight for your place at the King's Table? Do you think people have a plan to remove you? Are you always a victim? Do you blame others? I know it is hard to truly ask yourself those questions. If you are like me, and you are desperate for more than a promise of one day going to heaven, desperate to leave spiritual orphanhood behind, you will ask the hard questions and face the hard facts. What is the answer for this spiritual orphanhood? How is it healed? What's the cure? Is it to spend more time thinking about our past, our injustices, our unworthiness and depravity? It may seem a sign of deep faith to focus on our sin—but that's the enemy's spin. Satan, the accuser, wants us to believe we belong in Lo-debar. Our Dad invites us to His Table. He wants us to live as a son or daughter, in the Family, with all the benefits. It takes faith to live this way. Faith is the currency of heaven. You have to believe you are a son. It is by faith we are saved, it is by faith we receive Holy Spirit, it is by faith we learn to live with Him. Sons and daughters talk about who they are in Christ, and what He has done. Orphans talk about who they are *not* and what they have done. Spiritual orphans constantly want to earn approval. They want to satisfy their own appetites. They need others to constantly affirm them. They get their identity from the viewpoint of others.

Those of us who follow Christ will be tempted for the rest of our lives to follow Mephibosheth's lead and to drift back to Lo-debar. Throughout our lives, we tend to visit the King's Table on Sunday and drift back to Lo-debar the rest of the week. Then we drift back to the King's Table and do it all again. We get our fix on Sunday mornings, then we move back to orphan thinking. I don't want to live that way. I want to live my life at the King's Table. I want to be so determined to stay there that if someone tries to pull me away, I will simply not tolerate it. No one can pull me away without risking a punch to the face. I won't allow anything to make me return to Lo-debar. I will not leave the Table.

As you come up against Satan the accuser, you have to choose how you are going to view your life. Are you going to view your life based on your own thoughts, on what others say about you, on what the enemy says about you, or on what the Father says about you? The battle you will face for the rest of your life will be the battle between Lo-debar and the King's Table. It will be an ongoing fight to resist the pull to be more comfortable in Lo-debar than to remain at the Table. It seems noble, but it's not. At the King's Table, you hear the thoughts of your Father, the King, and all other voices grow dim. When you're sitting at the King's Table stuffing your face full of His food, and enjoying intimacy with Father, Son, and Holy Spirit, it's hard to hear the enemy. This makes it hard for me to understand why so many believers are so demon-centric. It's shocking how often I hear about what the enemy is doing in the lives of believers. Perhaps the enemy's voice is loud and clear because believers don't actually sit at the Table with their Father, Jesus, and Holy Spirit. Hearing the voice of the enemy constantly may not be a call to warfare intercession, it may be a sign that you've left the King's Table and returned to Lo-debar. You have allowed your thoughts to be permeated with lack.

One of the most amazing healings I have ever seen in my life was in Missouri when I prayed for a friend's knee. As I prayed for him, at least 50 flies started flying around his head. My friend received a miracle right in front of our eyes. His MCL and ACL were torn, and something in his ankle was torn. In front of our eyes, his knee began to shake when I commanded it to be whole. We watched what looked like a vein underneath his skin, from his ankle to his knee, move. It happened so fast that we were astonished. The enemy is more real than you think he is. He buzzes about like a fly, but he is just a maggot. The Father's Table always trumps that maggot. The accuser is under your feet. Why reach down, pull him up, eyeball-to-eyeball, and entertain his thoughts? I felt like I got born again, again when I came to my senses (Luke 15:17) and decided I wasn't going to make one more single excuse as to why I can't live in Eden the rest of my life while on this earth. I took responsibility for my own thoughts and my own life. It's more fun to be a friend of God than a victim of the enemy. Make your decision to get acclimated at the King's Table and receive the feast of intimacy with Him. You may be surprised at how fast you grow in your ability to hear the voice of your Father.

You belong.

Chapter 5

BELIEVING AND BELONGING

EVERYONE LONGS TO BELONG. In fact the need to belong is so strong that people will do almost anything to satisfy it. Young people join violent gangs out of a need to belong. Many who are involved in the occult got to that dark place out of a sense of rejection, of not belonging. Our need to belong seems to be part of our DNA, perhaps because God designed us to belong to Him, to His family. He made a place for us at His Table before the foundations of the world. Satan is always busy trying to get us away from our place at the Table. To get to the King's Table and stay there, we must believe what God has said. The message of the Kingdom is not to say "yes" to heaven, it is to say "yes" to the King.

He is our Lord, our creator, and more than that, He has invited us into His family. In God's family, Jesus is our Big Brother. He isn't just the bridge to heaven, He's the bridge to the Father. When you understand and embrace these truths you realize that the invitation is to come and enjoy God, to walk with Him in the cool of the day—to just be with Him. When is the last time you just enjoyed God? Wouldn't you like to spend your life enjoying God rather than wondering every day if He even likes you? You can, if you believe.

When you truly believe that His Table is your home, you get to experience things in the Kingdom that others don't. The supernatural becomes natural to you—and you live in thankfulness for the place you have at the Table. It's not a place of arrogance. It's a place of belonging. I know this because I've lived it. I've lived in Lo-debar and I do not want to go back. I spent much of my life hating God because I did not understand Him. I have to tell you—I am no longer Mephibosheth. I am not in Lo-debar. I am God's child. I don't say this because I am a pastor. I don't even let my church call me "pastor." I'm just Chad. I sit at the Table because it's where I belong. This is home to me now. My goal for you is that you will leave Lo-debar and come home. Come to your place at the Table.

Living at home at the Table means things that once would have seemed strange and impossible become the usual. Imagine that an angel manifests to you and instead of being terrified, you calmly say, "How's it going?" I'm not kidding. This is life at the King's Table. Dramatic things can happen to you spiritually and not catch you off guard. What if your eyes were trained so that the realm of the supernatural was more real than what you can see, feel, or taste? Imagine you own your own business and business is not going well. You've had four prophetic words in the past month about how well your business is going to go. When the King's Table is home, instead of falling apart, you can hang onto the Word of God, believing in Him. We need to understand that the Word from the Lord is more real than the bank account that is precariously close to zero dollars. It is more real than our lack. How do we go about believing in God? It's a learning process. You begin to trust Him beyond your own understanding, and as you do, He becomes your reality.

It is awesome when things manifest as He promised and instead of being shocked, you think, "Well, that is what You said would happen, Father." This is how Jesus responded to Satan in the desert. He repeatedly referenced the Word He believed. Over and over He responded to Satan beginning with the words "It is written." The same naturally supernatural lifestyle that Jesus lives at the King's Table is possible for all sons and daughters of the King. We don't have to live like spiritual orphans. We can move beyond doubt to belief and take our place at the Table of the King.

EMBRACING HEAVEN'S CULTURE

When confronted with doubt, spiritual orphans say, "You are so right, it is so true." Spiritual sons say, "hush." Waiting for doubt to leave is ridiculous. You don't wait for it to leave—you tell it to hush. Chapter 1 in the gospel of Luke is a good place to see the difference between doubt, which is a characteristic of a spiritual orphan, and belief, which is a characteristic of a spiritual son or daughter. Please understand, there's nothing wrong with doubt as long as you don't yield to it. Faith is not the absence of doubt. Faith is looking at doubt, punching it in the face and moving towards the truth. If you wait until there's no doubt, you will be waiting for Jesus Christ to come back. He will split the sky open and you will be sitting there saying, "wait a minute."

In Luke 1:5-25 we meet Zechariah, who was a priest in the lineage of Abijah, and his wife Elizabeth who was barren. He and his wife were very old, and both were righteous in the sight of God, observing all His commands and decrees blamelessly. Being a priest, he had a strong history with God and was very familiar with Him. Simply put, God liked this guy. On this particular day, Zechariah was serving as a priest before God. He was chosen, according to the custom of the priesthood, to go to the temple of the Lord and burn incense. When the time for the burning of incense came, all the assembled worshipers were praying outside. This was not just a few people showing up for church. This was a big deal. Zechariah went in, and they were all outside waiting to see what would happen. No one expected what happened next. An angel of the Lord appeared to Zechariah, standing at the right side of the altar of incense.

Think about this for a minute. God released an angel to personally deliver a message to Zechariah, a righteous man who had a history with God and was very familiar with Him. Isn't it a bit odd that someone so familiar with God, who had been around the ways of God for so long (remember Zechariah was old) would react the way he did—with doubt? The angel delivered 11 amazing promises to Zechariah. "Your wife Elizabeth will bear you a son, and you are to call him John. He will be a joy and a delight to you, and many will rejoice because of his birth, for he will be great in the sight of the Lord. He is never to take wine or other fermented drink, and he will be filled with the Holy Spirit even before he is born. He will bring back many of the people of Israel to the Lord their God. And he will go on before the Lord, in the spirit and power of Elijah, to turn the hearts of the parents to their children and the disobedient to the wisdom of the righteous—to make ready a people prepared for the Lord" (Luke 1:13-17). That's a lot of promises. How many more promises does a righteous man need to hear? You'd think Zechariah would have jumped for joy and thankfulness. Yet, in the very next verse, he asked the angel, "How can I be sure of this? I am an old man and my wife is well along in years" (Luke 1:18). He doubted the word. We know that we are growing in deep friendship with God when an encounter happens, or a strong word is given, and we believe what the Father is saying regardless of how this affects our natural senses. We simply default to childlike belief.

Jesus was the perfect example of someone who lived believing what the Father said. In fact He only did what He saw the Father doing, only said what He heard the Father saying. When He raised Lazarus from the grave, He didn't even pray for him. Instead, He said, "Father this is for You, not for Me." Then He simply said, "Get up." (See John 11:41-42) When a little boy from a crowd of 5,000 handed Jesus a few fish and loaves of bread, Jesus was just messing with Philip when He said, "Where shall we buy bread for these people to eat?" (John 6:5). He already knew His Father would provide more than enough. He wasn't mortified by anything down here on earth. People were constantly plotting to kill Him, but He was so connected to Father that even constant death threats didn't impact the way He operated.

You know where you are in relation to Lo-debar based upon your reaction to the manifestations of the Kingdom of God. Why are we so shocked when someone is healed? Why are we so shocked when someone gets delivered? Why are we so shocked when the presence of God fills the room and we literally cannot stand up under the power? It should be so common. For Zechariah, it didn't happen that way. Many times, it doesn't happen that way for us, either. If you're wondering where you are on the scale between Lo-debar and the King's Table, ask yourself this question: "When you are squeezed in a "suddenly moment," what comes out?" What are suddenly moments? The gospels and the book of Acts are full of suddenly moments—moments when the unexpected happens and people must react immediately. You can gauge where you are with God when a suddenly moment happens. If you squeeze an orange, apple juice doesn't come out. Yet, when you squeeze a born-again Christian, many times, more of the enemy than the Kingdom comes out. If I squeeze you in Lo-debar, then Lo-debar comes out. If I squeeze you at the King's Table, sonship will come out.

Spiritual orphans are always dominated by what they can see, taste, touch, feel, and hear. Those at the King's Table trust His Word no matter what the natural says, because the Word matters more than what we can taste, touch, feel, and hear. This is why Paul says, in Colossians 3:1-3, to set your heart and mind on things above. What if heaven's culture was more real to you than the earth? It can happen if you will fight through doubt with faith, and believe.

Let's return to Zechariah. Gabriel showed up and Zechariah was thrown into doubt. In a suddenly moment he wasn't able to set his mind on things above. Zechariah asked the angel, "How can I be sure of this?" He was actually talking to a mighty angel of God and giving into unbelief. This did not make Gabriel or God very happy. "I am Gabriel," was the response. "I stand in the presence of God, and I have been sent to speak to you and to tell you this good news. And now you will be silent and not able to speak until the day this happens, because you did not believe my words, which will come true at their appointed time" (Luke 1:19-20). I can just imagine Gabriel taking his sword and putting it right up to Zechariah's nose and saying something like, "You do *not* want to say this to Jehovah." You see, God values your belief. He wants you to believe and receive what's at His Table, not doubt it and do without for the rest of your life. Orphans will focus on their doubt while sons push past their doubt and believe. It isn't that sons are more favored or holy, it's simply that they believe. They counter doubt with faith. Without faith, it is impossible to believe. Living in that place of "in all faith believing" takes courage.

So, what is faith? Many believers struggle to understand it. We already know that faith is not the absence of doubt. Faith is punching doubt right in the face and continuing to move forward. Faith is believing God and taking Him at His Word no matter what the natural realm says. Faith says, "No one is taking me off my place at the Table—no angels, no demons, no nothing." When you're living in faith at the King's Table, you don't need a great man or woman of God to anoint you. You were anointed at Calvary. All you have to do is agree with Calvary. To the degree you agree with Calvary, you lock onto the truth. When you lock onto the truth you will find yourself being wooed to the Table and eventually, it will feel like home. When you're solidly at home with God you don't get easily shaken. If someone gives you a bizarre prophetic word, you don't fall apart. Instead, you say, "Thank you so much for giving me that word, but that's not from Father. I don't judge you. I love you." An orphan's response is different. When an orphan hears a bizarre word, their response is, "Ugghhh, destruction is coming to me." In contrast, sons and daughters say, "Surely goodness and mercy shall follow me all the days of my life." I'm encouraging you to exercise your faith for yourself, to make God's truths so personal that you literally believe you're as close to the heart of Father as Jesus was while He was here. I'm talking about believing. I love how Luke didn't spend too much time focusing on Zechariah's doubts. The gospel narrative goes on to tell us that even though Zechariah doubted, Elizabeth got pregnant, just as promised. The truth is, God keeps His promises.

RESPONDING TO GOD'S PURSUIT

Zechariah and Elizabeth were not the only ones who experienced a suddenly moment that demanded a faith response. There was also Mary. Mary was a very young girl. Biblical scholars estimate her age to be about 13 or 14 years old. She was a young girl from a no-name town in the middle of nowhere, called Nazareth. God being no respecter of persons sent Gabriel to this desolate location with the most astounding and impactful message the world has ever known. "In the sixth month of Elizabeth's pregnancy, God sent the angel Gabriel to Nazareth, a town in Galilee, to a virgin pledged to be married to a man named Joseph, a descendant of David. The virgin's name was Mary. The angel went to her and said, 'Greetings, you who are highly favored! The Lord is with you.' Mary was greatly troubled at his words and wondered what kind of greeting this might be" (Luke 1:26-29). Mary was troubled by the magnitude of the good news, not the news itself. Zechariah was full of doubt. Mary was full of faith and incredulous all at the same time. Often, when God shows up, those who don't know His true nature expect that He just wants to rough them up or teach them a lesson. Imagine if an angel manifested to you and just said, "Father loves you so much"? Remember the angel that appeared to Cornelius and simply said, "Your prayers and gifts to the poor have come up as a memorial offering before God" (Acts 10:4). A paraphrase of that verse is "God really likes you." These kinds of suddenly moments are amazing, especially when people respond with faith.

Gabriel brought *the* Good News and Mary responded in faith. "But the angel said to her, "Do not be afraid, Mary; you have found favor with God. You will conceive and give birth to a son, and you are to call him Jesus. He will be great and will be called the Son of the Most High. The Lord God will give him the throne of His father David" (Luke 1:30-32). Can you even imagine the magnitude of these words for Mary? This was a huge message, delivered pretty matter-of-factly by Gabriel. I love how, to God, things down here are just not a big deal. That is the whole story of the Bible. God was always using ordinary, unexpecting people to do extraordinary and amazing things, even things that seemed impossible. Here is a nugget to hold onto. God chooses us. He's the one doing the choosing. Our choice becomes simple. It's either yes or no. There is no other option, just yes or no.

One of the things I have noticed is how many times God pursues people for an assignment. In Genesis 12:1-3, Abram was not praying that God would show up and ask him to be the father of a nation. As a matter of fact, he was living in a polytheistic society and culture, and there is a great chance Abram was not aware of Jehovah's identity. He likely didn't know who God was. Think on that for a minute. It was God's idea to initiate a relationship and assignment with Abram. Then there was Moses who was on the backside of a desert when God showed up in a burning bush. (See Exodus 3:1-17) Moses never saw this coming, which continues to show me why Richard Foster calls God, "The great hound of heaven" (Prayer: Finding the Heart's True Home, 70). Jesus is the one who finds Andrew and tells him to go to his brother Simon Peter. (See John 1:41) Once again God takes the initiative and people have to decide what to do in response.

I don't know what large words you have been given over your life, but nothing can compare to the words given to and received by Mary. Let's look more closely at how she handled it. She basically said, "Okay—well, how will this be? I am a virgin." (See Luke 1:34) I love her response. It's certainly not full of doubt. Sometimes, when God shows up and you know it's Him, you need to just go ahead and believe before you take time to overanalyze the word being given to you. If Mary had processed this word for too long, doubt could have crept in. She could have thought, "Wait a minute. God is going to be in my belly? God? No!" Mary didn't overanalyze in the natural. She just received in her Spirit what God was saying.

Gabriel wasn't finished. He continued, "The Holy Spirit will come on you, and the power of the Most High will overshadow you. So the holy one to be born will be called the Son of God" (Luke 1:35). There's never been another message on this earth to a human being from God bigger than this message. Just look at Mary's response: "I am the Lord's servant," Mary answered. "May your word to me be fulfilled" (Luke 1:38). She basically said, "Sounds good to me. I'm all in." The very same angel, Gabriel, appeared to both Zechariah and Mary. Both received astounding words that seemed impossible in the natural. One said, "I just don't believe it." The other said, "Well, let it be done to me as you have spoken." You may be thinking, "No one ever prophesies over me. What word, exactly, am I supposed to believe?"

Are you ready? Let me prophesy over you. How about this for a prophetic word:

- John 1:12: *"Yet to all who did receive Him, to those who believed in his name, He gave the right to become children of God . . ."* Do you believe it?

- Ephesians 1:5: *". . . he predestined us for adoption to sonship through Jesus Christ, in accordance with his pleasure and will . . ."* Do you believe it?

- Romans 15:7: *"Accept one another, then, just as Christ accepted you, [just as Christ brought you to his King's table], in order to bring praise to God."* Do you believe it?

- 1 Corinthians 6:17: *"But whoever is united with the Lord is one with him in spirit."* Do you believe it?

- Colossians 1:21-22: *"Once you were alienated from God and were enemies in your minds because of your evil behavior [in Lo-debar]. But now he has reconciled you [he's bridged you] by Christ's physical body through death to present you holy in his sight, without blemish and free from accusation . . ."* Do you believe it ?

RECEIVING THE WHITE ROBE

My friend Justin had a major breakthrough when He finally believed one of these truths. I met Justin eight years ago, when he was a landscaper in Greenville, South Carolina. I wanted him to give me a quote for some landscaping we wanted done at our house. In our first meeting, a 30-minute quote turned into a 4-hour prophetic prayer time. On my back porch, the Lord began to show me things about Justin's life that were quite dramatic. The power of the prophetic is that the Holy Spirit opens up doors in one minute to show what sometimes takes years to discover by doing life with someone. To say that Justin and I bonded during that time on my back porch is putting it lightly. This began a six-year discipling relationship. I invited Justin into my life and began to invest a lot of time in helping him develop a paradigm of what it looks like to pursue Jesus with every inch of one's being.

A year into our time together, Justin shared with me that he was having a really difficult time hearing God at all. It was driving him crazy. He was getting tired of not being able to hear the voice of his shepherd. (See John 10:27) I decided to meet with him at Cracker Barrel. I love meeting over food, and thought that a nice, relaxing southern meal would put Justin in a great place to receive a challenging word from me. When we sat down, I said, "Justin, I am not going to leave this restaurant until you get a word from God for me. Time is up. It's time for you to start operating at a high level in the prophetic." He stared at me like something was wrong with me. A couple of hours passed, and Justin was not hearing anything. He was frustrated. So was I. We finally had to give up and leave the restaurant without a breakthrough.

That night Justin went to bed. In one dream, everything changed for him. In his dream, the Lord walked up to him and said, "You want to know why you can't hear Me like Chad does?" Then the Lord showed Justin that he was dressed in a filthy garment that was gross. Justin looked at what he was dressed in and realized that it was dirty. Then the Lord handed him a robe that was pure white. The Lord said to him, "When you see yourself dressed in white like this and truly believe that you are clean in My eyes, you will hear Me."

Over the last five years, I have been around very few people more prophetic than Justin. He went from not being able to hear God to hearing Him a mile a minute. It all changed with one simple principle: until you see yourself as being as clean as Jesus, you will never walk in a high level of the prophetic. It is practically impossible to be naturally supernatural if you see yourself as dirty in the Father's eyes. In other words, you cannot pull your chair up to the King's Table, and stay there, if you don't believe. Justin had to believe Colossians 1:21-22. He had to believe that, thanks to Jesus, he literally is pure and blameless before God. Truly believing Colossians 1:21-22 is more powerful than getting someone to pray a prayer of impartation over you. I have seen people go from thinking God hates them to truly believing they are clean in His eyes. And wouldn't you know, they begin to see healing manifest when they pray for people. They began to be the one to encourage others with prophetic words.

Jesus gives lots of words, but very few people actually believe them. I am telling you, come sit at the Table and stay at the Table. You don't need a pastor to hug every Sunday morning. You don't need someone to affirm you nine times, just so you can get through the day. Take one passage and, for once in your life, decide to sit at the Table and stay at the Table. No matter what is happening in your life, you can stay connected to the Table because you believe God's Word. Others may ask, "How can you be so confident when it doesn't seem like things are going great in your life?" The answer is: "Because I believe God more than my circumstances."

Bottom line for my life: I would rather sit at His Table and have my life look like Lo-debar, than to have material abundance, but a soul full of Lo-debar. Isn't it interesting that in the middle of suffering Paul kept saying, "I just want to know you, I just want to know you." At His Table, even suffering produces the sweet aroma of intimacy. It may seem like everything's falling apart in my life, but I have something other people don't have. I've got sonship. I've got a Father. Lo-debar is no longer a place I want to be. So even when life gets tough, it doesn't force me away from the Table. I continue to dig into His Word and believe His Truths.

When I open the Word to just discover how good it is, I can grow more in six months than six years. If I'm studying to get to the King's Table, then I've already lost. If I believe I am already at the King's Table, and I am studying to realize what this means, then it makes sense to me when

David says, "You prepare a table before me in the presence of my enemies" (Psalm 23:5). The Table doesn't give me immunity from spiritual warfare, it just equips me to take naps in the storms and wonder why other people are flipping out so much.

The King's Table is a good place to dwell. If you are tired of making your abode in Lo-debar, then get out. Don't be a string-bound elephant. Have you seen them? They are huge elephants who just sit there, not moving, because they are attached to a string, a little bitty string tied around a small 2 x 4 on the ground. When I see this, I want to say to the elephant, "You have the power to kill a village and you just sit right there. Just pull the thing out of the ground, just pull the thing out." If your thoughts are keeping you in the suburbs of Lo-debar, get some new thoughts. As Paul would say, "Quit drinking the milk, quit blaming your pastor who 15 years ago looked at you wrong, quit blaming the teacher who said you were ugly." We've all been hurt. We can all build libraries of doubt based upon our own experiences. Every once in a while, someone says, "I believe that word even if it never manifests." Then, they obey based on that truth. That's faith. It is an amazing experience. Think about where you are in relation to Lo-debar and the King's Table. Is it time for an about-face, to begin thinking like God thinks? Is it time to know the truth and act on it? Is it time to punch doubt in the face and keep moving forward? Is it time to believe?

CHASING THE FATHER'S HEART

Have you ever asked what the Father wants from you? You will spend eternity with Him in heaven. The question we need to ask is, "What does He want here?" Let's begin with this—you are part of His family. He wants to do what families do, which is to enjoy being together. He wants to connect with you, to talk to you about things that you don't even think are that important. Spiritual orphans only go to God when crisis is on the line. Sons say, "Father, what is on your mind?"

Recently, as we were about to leave on vacation, a sister of mine from our church prayed over me. As soon as she began praying, Holy Spirit said, "Listen to her." She said I had a very large assignment during our time away. I wasn't being called to minister, and I wasn't being called to speak. My first thought was, "Thank you, Father, I love those kind of assignments."

All I had packed was one pair of shorts, three shirts, a bathing suit and a pre-season college football magazine. Not exactly what you would wear if you were planning on blessing people. The grocery store was a tenth of a mile from our condo. All I planned to do was eat, stare at the ocean, and hangout with my wife and kids. The very thought of it felt like heaven to me. I knew the assignment that week was for my wife and me to connect on a deep level, to have lots of conversations. And we did. We talked all week, and experienced a significant breakthrough. As a matter of fact, I don't remember having a week like that since we've been married. Our kids were there, there were no mediators, we were not reading any Christian books. I wasn't listening to teaching on marital interests. I love all that, but we just talked.

Then, I went for a walk on the beach and Father said, "Chad, because of your obedience to your assignment for this week, you have already opened doors for yourself that you know nothing of." I was walking from the condo and I asked, "What do you mean?" He answered, "So many people misunderstand Me. I'm not a pushover. When I give someone an assignment in the Kingdom, I'm a rewarder of their obedience. I want you to start teaching how I'm a rewarder." You see, God doesn't play favorites. He doesn't just say, "Reward that one, don't reward that one." He wants us to believe and obey. Paul tells us multiple times that we should lean into obedience. Orphans always have a reason, an excuse as to why they can't be obedient, and why they just don't have it in them. A son or daughter says, "Lord, what is it you want with me? My life is yours. I have no right to the Table. I am grateful to be at the Table. I just want to be with You, to enjoy You. I'll do whatever You ask because I love You and want to please You." Blessings manifest when you go after the heart of Father, not after the heart of the blessing. If you're fulfilling an assignment to get blessed, you're missing the whole point. Fulfill the assignment because you're chasing Father's heart.

Chapter 6

LIFE IN THE PROMISED LAND

I HAVE NO IDEA how I am going to die. I'd love to meet the King of Kings dramatically like Elijah did. Or perhaps drop dead as an old man preaching one more time in some remote village somewhere. It would be incredible to go out like that. I often wonder how I am going to catch the big red wagon out of here. Only He knows. But I can tell you, right now, three ways that I won't die: I will not be eaten by a shark, die in a small airplane, or die shopping with my wife.

My family and friends have heard me say something like, "I would not get on a small airplane if Jesus Christ manifested in the flesh and demanded that I do it" at least a hundred times in my life. I like flying about as much as I like the idea of getting attacked by a large dog on my neck, but I do it all the time. I'm actually writing this chapter on an airplane. I don't enjoy flying at all, but I can at least manage my anxiety on a 777 with too much food and a sports page to read. But small planes? No way. I'm a bold man who will step out in faith with the best of them, but when that step of faith is boarding a Cessna, this guy is not interested. I don't care what a little plane's history is, how the engines were built, how fun the flight can be, or who is passionate about it. Don't talk about it with me. Sometimes I'm around people who say, "I love Cessnas. They are so fun to fly—you zip around in the air." I respond, "I specialize in deliverance ministry if you are interested." Man is not meant to climb into a container smaller than a glove compartment of a Honda Civic and go up into the air.

Little did I know…

My friend Steve Keyes called me about a trip to Arizona, and it sounded like a great deal to me. Steve is one of the pastors of the church I lead, and he is like a father figure in my life. The Lord put it on his heart to surprise me and take me to Arizona to play golf. I've played golf my entire life, and I'm always interested in a golf trip. A month before Steve called me, I had a dream that I was playing golf in Arizona. God gave me a heads-up that something fun was coming down the pike. I had no clue that both Steve and God were playing a trick on me. If you don't think God has a sense of humor, you don't know Him well. He does, trust me.

Before the trip, Steve told me that he wanted us to visit the Grand Canyon. I was excited because I had never seen it, and I've heard my whole life how majestic and awe-inspiring it is. I've seen many pictures of the Grand Canyon, and I was really excited about getting to see it for myself. Steve and I were going on a road trip—God's two little helpers enjoying some golf and the Grand Canyon. When we landed in Phoenix I was really happy because I always enjoy getting off of an airplane. While I get gassy, antsy, and nauseous boarding a plane, as I exit the aircraft I feel like I've just done a detox—happy and healthy. So, I breathed the warm Arizona air. We made our way to our first golf course. About two miles from the first tee box, Steve said, "That's where we fly out tomorrow to go to the Grand Canyon." The last time I had a feeling come over me like the one that came over me in that moment was during the last exam I took at the University of Georgia. I had to make a 77 on an anthropology exam to graduate. I did not even know what anthropology was, even after a whole semester, but I knew I had to make a 77. I felt sick taking that test. It was the exact same feeling when I saw tiny paper airplanes taking off from the Sedona Airport. I stared a hole in Steve's eyes for 30 seconds. I can't write what I said to Steve next, because this book would not be published. Let's just say that I was not a happy man. I said, "Steve, are you telling me that we are flying to the Grand Canyon on a small plane?" He said, "Yes, and then we are going to get on a helicopter that is glassed in and take it over the canyon."

I could not feel anything on my left side for the next 20 minutes. I was numb, hopeless, and lost. Steve thought all this was hysterical. He kept saying, "You'll have such great memories to share with other people!" I responded, "I don't care about other people right now, Steve." What made matters worse was the fact that Sedona was experiencing unusual wind during that week. The wind blew so hard during our rounds of golf that it was hard to even play some of the holes. I thought the wind was blowing hard on the golf course—until I was introduced to true wind when we arrived at the airport.

LEARNING TO LIVE WITH COURAGE

The next morning we arrived at that little demonic airport with all its little demonic paper airplanes waiting on the runway for us. I walked into the tiny closet main desk area and met a man named Bob who was standing behind the counter. Bob introduced himself as our pilot. I sized him up like a prizefighter at a weigh-in. He asked me a couple of questions, but I did not hear him because I was getting some words of knowledge over him from the Holy Spirit to make sure that this guy knew what he was doing. While Steve filled out our paperwork, I walked outside to talk to God. I needed to chat. When I walked outside, the wind was blowing 30 mph. That is not "preacher talk" exaggeration at all. You can contact Steve Keyes and ask him for yourself. The wind was blowing so hard that I genuinely thought they might cancel the flight. They had actually canceled all flights the day before. I prayed in tongues for three minutes that the flight would cancel. But it did not.

As I sat on a bench outside, I noticed that the bench was a memorial in honor of a young lady who lost her life at this airport as a pilot. It was a somber moment for me that made me think deeply about my own life. I sat on this bench, thinking through my biggest fear and what was about to happen. I said, "Father, I don't like this. I know where I'm going when it's over, I just don't like this." He immediately responded, "Chad, who do you think gave Steve this idea? Who do you think planned it on this day? Chad, I'm the one behind this. I want you to face your biggest fear." I sat there for a few more minutes and said, "OK. If this is what you want, I'll do it."

When I say that the wind was blowing, I don't want you to think wind. Imagine more of a cyclone-tornado type onslaught. I kid you not, this seasoned pilot sent by the Almighty to make me face my biggest fear said when we got in the plane, "It is whipping today. Unusual for this time of year." I could sense God smiling over me.

Steve and I met a newlywed couple on the flight, and the groom was as nervous as I was. I was not in the mood for small talk, and neither was he. We were more uncomfortable than two wet black cats under a ladder. It took a few minutes for the plane to warm up after Bob started it using the same motion I use to I start my leaf blower. That plane sounded like a 90-year-old golfer warming up for 36 holes on a cold day. Going down the runway, I noticed that my feet were absolutely soaking my flip-flops. I was sweating out all sorts of toxins, fear, and agoraphobia. The takeoff was not like what you experience on a regular plane. Nothing I've ever done could prepare me for what it was like. We shot up into the sky fast, and in a bad mood. For the next hour, I was the most miserable I have ever been on this earth—or, technically, above this earth. I've had some dark days before, and I know what it is like to walk through clinical depression, but I have never experienced acute anxiety like I did on that tiny plane. I talked to God more in that one hour than I had in the previous three months.

Halfway through the flight Bob said, "If you look to the right, you will see the highest elevated city in Arizona and there is still some snow on top of the mountain." Steve and the bride in the back seat were enthralled with the scenery, history, landscape, and majesty of Arizona. The groom and I couldn't care less. We wanted that flying minivan to just get on the ground. To make matters worse, I did not hear God say one single thing the entire flight. I talk to God all the time and share whatever is going on with me. It's not unusual for me to hear Him over the most trivial matters. But when I wanted to hear from Him the most, I heard nothing. Not one single thing.

I sat so close to Bob that I thought he was going to ask me to help him fly the plane. My knees were crammed in that cockpit like Pringles in a can. We had earphones on and communicated through a little microphone. I kept asking him, "Is this wind normal?" I tried to act as casual as possible, but I knew that he recognized that I was terrified. He never said one single thing that calmed me down. Like God, Bob wasn't into talking that day either.

When that plane landed, I did not celebrate at all. I knew what awaited us. The groom and I complained during our entire death march to the helicopter. If you think flying in a Cessna in a 30 mph wind is miserable, try getting into a helicopter. I went from panic attack and hot flashes to a literal fear of death. I've seen people healed of many different things as a result of prayer and different types of miracles, and I've had three open visions in my life. None of that mattered in this moment. My relationship with God seemed distant at my greatest time of need. Steve must have told me five times we would be OK. But I kept saying two things, 1) "Don't touch me." 2) "Quit speaking to me."

The groom and I climbed into the helicopter. All I could see was glass. I felt like I was in a huge see-through bowl. I thought I had a phobia of little planes, but God made sure I knew there was something worse. We took off in this helicopter and shot straight up as the groom and I stared at a hole into the seat in front of us. Meanwhile, Steve and the bride were as happy as two little June bugs in the South Georgia sunshine. We flew low over the trees for about a mile and then I saw something from a distance that made my bowels and knees literally weak.

When we got near the Grand Canyon, our pilot said, "Hang on." I'm telling you right now that I prayed that God would snatch us up like Enoch. I seriously wanted to die and get out of that helicopter by simply disappearing into heaven like Elijah. We dropped what seemed like 54 miles. As I looked down, I could not feel my tongue. I don't know if you have ever been to the Grand Canyon before, but it is impossible to describe. When God made the Grand Canyon, I imagine Him saying, "Let's do something that will make them go into shock when they see it." It is absolutely stunning and overwhelming. Especially when you are in a glass helicopter with a pilot that was playing Led Zeppelin. You can't make this stuff up. If I were the pilot, I would pass out Zoloft and play Barry Manilow songs to calm people down. Not this guy. He was playing music one level above "Welcome to The Jungle" by Guns 'N' Roses. With all that going on, I didn't really even want to see the Canyon. That hour in the 'copter seemed to last a month.

At one point I glanced down and noticed that the Colorado River in the Canyon looked like a tiny one-inch wide creek. That is the point where the groom touched my shoulder and said, "I want to get off of this helicopter." I wish I could tell you that at some point, I simply recited Psalm 91, reclined onto the shoulder of Jesus, and relaxed in His presence. I did not. I death-gripped the leather seat in front of me and waited it out until we landed. When we landed, I had a whopping 20 minutes to rest until we got back into the paper airplane with Bob and headed back to Sedona. The flight back was just as bad. I have never in my life been happier to get back to a hotel room. As a matter of fact, I paid for Steve and me to get professional massages in this resort town just to get me back to neutral.

As the months passed after God made me face my biggest fear, I came to realize that He was the one behind this experience all along. A friend once told me that it's easier to see what God was doing in your past than to detect what He is doing in your present and future. That has proven true for me many times. Since that trip, God has led me to lead the merger between two churches and two elder boards, to cast a unique vision to a staff, change the names of two churches into one, and introduce this idea of being a church that stands in between the Spirit and the Word. It's been a journey without any room for fear. That flight over the Canyon helped prepare me to live with courage. It taught me how everything I am able to do comes from my dependency on the Father. No way would I ever have had, or survived, that experience on my own. But He knew what I needed to learn in order to do what I needed to do. Because I was depending on Him, I got to learn it, and do it. God is not a teddy bear. He is not afraid to push us to do things we did not think we were capable of doing. I know now that He made me get on that plane for a reason.

Getting on that plane required a lot of courage on my part. I had to face my fears and trust Bob. I had to trust the Cessna, then the helicopter. I had to trust that Bob, the pilot, knew what he was doing. I even had to trust that Bob knew where to go, how to get us there and back. I did not trust me. I could not put my trust in my emotions, my intellect and reasoning skills, my degrees, my bank account or even my own experiences. I had to be totally dependent on this stranger that I had just met. I had to trust that he knew what he was doing. Trust is earned. It is not guaranteed. Even in the Kingdom trust is important. Even if you are at the Table. Even when you know you are a Son. Trust takes time.

LIFE IN THE PROMISED LAND

People respond differently to fear. My grandmother ran. She lived in one of those houses built in the fifties that had closets that are 6 miles long. Today we have walk-in-closets so big you could raise a family in them. There is something in me that loves to scare people. I would hide in my grandmother's closet in the mornings and when she opened that door to get her shoes, she would see me and take off running, no screams, no nothing. She would just take off running like Usain Bolt, in his prime. My sister falls apart. She took piano lessons and one of my favorite things to do was to sneak up on her while she was practicing and just yell right into her ear. Some people get angry. Those people will chase you with a cast iron frying pan - that's my wife. Some people freeze. They cannot move at all, they cannot speak.

Fear does strange things to people. We all have fears. Faith is not an absence of fear. Faith is trusting God, and God is love. The greatest command is to love God and love others. There is no greater love than that we lay down our lives for another. Perfect love drives out fear. That is the truth, right out of the Word. Faith doesn't drive out fear, love does. If you want to live a life of freedom from fear, we go to the Word. As I have said before, we tend to change our thoughts to fit the truth. We keep telling ourselves the truth while it is what God says that is the truth. It is not my emotions, my intellect or reasoning skills, my opinions, my five senses, and it is not my experiences that are the truth. What God says is the truth. He is trustworthy. Over and over in the Word we see Him described as good, as loving and merciful, and as kind. Even when you are sitting in a Cessna drenched in your own cold sweat, trying with all your might to hear from Him, He is worthy of your trust, because He is love.

Again, God is not a teddy bear. He is not my buddy, my hombre, my bro. He is God. He is LORD. That means master, owner. He will test you to see if you are trustworthy. You can expect tests. Peter did. He denied knowing Jesus three times, but then on the day of Pentecost, less than two months later, Peter stood before all the Jews (in Acts 2) and spoke the truth. "You killed Jesus, He arose and is with Father, and now you have the opportunity to repent. And by the way, this is what Joel prophesied. Now we have the Helper, the Power, the Comforter, with us. Oh yeah, remember the pillar of fire our fathers followed? Well it is now dispersed and on the heads of many, not just the priests. It's on everyone." Wow! What changed? How did Peter change from being scared of a young girl to standing before the leaders of his people? How did Peter move from doubt and fear to the power and wisdom to speak with boldness and authority? Was it love? Jesus asked him three times, do you love me, and Peter said "yes." Just loving Him isn't enough. Just knowing you are loved is not enough. There is more. More good news. The Gospel is more than just knowing Jesus, saying a prayer when you were 10 years old. The Gospel is the gospel of the Kingdom. The good news is that we do not have to wait until the sweet by and by, just tolerating our time on earth until we get up there to the Promised Land. This here right now is the Promised Land. This is eternal life. It has already started. It is not a future wish. You are not a scared kid. You are a Son of the Living God, the Most High, the King of Kings, the Lord of Lords. And that is awesome.

Holy Spirit came. He is in us. He is with us. He empowers us. With Him we are more than conquerors; with Him we can do all things. With Him we can heal the sick, cleanse the lepers and cast out demons. With Him we can love well. With Him we can expand our hearts to love more. We can begin to see through His eyes. With Him we can hear directly from Him because He talks to us. With Him we can change our thought patterns to think like Him. He came to show us that love looks like something. As John Wimber said, "We all get to play." The only way you are left out is if you choose not to play.

KINGDOM AUTHORITY

In Matthew, chapter 4 we find Jesus beginning His public ministry with baptism in the Jordan by His cousin, John the Baptist. John, the son of Elizabeth and Zechariah, was the fulfillment of the promise that was delivered to Zechariah by the angel Gabriel. He grew up to be just who Gabriel prophesied he would be. He became a forerunner who went before the Lord, filled with the Holy Spirit from birth, to restore many of the people of Israel back to the Lord, their God. He carried the power of Elijah to turn the hearts of parents back to their children, and the disobedient to the wisdom of righteousness. He prepared the people as the prophets did prior to the new order established by Jesus. John's ministry was one of restoration back into the order established by Moses. When John baptized Jesus, as He came out of the water, the Holy Spirit came like a dove alighting on Him before leading Him into the wilderness for 40 days of fasting. Those 40 days were not all popsicles and sunshine. Jesus was tempted. How did He respond? With truth, with the Word of God. Not by argument or reasoning, or manipulation. Jesus responded to the enemy with "It is written" on three separate occasions in Matthew 4. Jesus then left the desert and headed to Capernaum where He began to preach. This is the first record of His public ministry. His first words are recorded in Matthew 4:17, "Repent for the Kingdom of heaven has come near." The first words from our Lord Jesus's mouth were not "believe in me." They are not "bow down to me." They are not "love me." The first words make no mention of being born again. The first word out of Jesus' mouth was "metanoia," which in Greek means "to change the way you think." In other words, Jesus was saying, "Start thinking like Me. Start thinking the thoughts of your King. Change the way you think because I am bringing the Kingdom of heaven here. It is a new order." Notice that Jesus didn't say that *He* was going to change the way we are to think. The change part is our responsibility. Jesus was putting first things first in His inaugural speech. God is all about first's. He honored Abel for giving the first and best of his crops as a sacrifice, but found Cain's offerings unacceptable because he did not give the firsts. Paying attention to firsts is important.

Honestly though, how do we know what to think? God's Word tells us what to think. Without the Word of God, and the revelation of Father's love for you and others, without Jesus putting a face on God so we could see an example of Father, we can spend a lifetime like a hamster just running on a wheel, working hard at going nowhere. Without an understanding of the Kingdom of God and the help of Holy Spirit, we are in trouble. Breaking the orphan spirit and recognizing your position at the Table with the Father includes understanding Kingdom authority along with Kingdom identity. We need both in the fruitful Christian life.

THE NARROW GATE

The enemy of your soul is slick and crafty, so crafty that he can rile up a passion in you that is misdirected towards a false belief of Jesus instead of the truth of the Kingdom. Let me give you an example. People often say, "Yes, I believe that Jesus died on a cross so that I can get to heaven when I die. I am going to try to stay clean and talk to more people so they can believe that too." Satan believes that too. We give messages that focus on Jesus dying on the cross and then ask people if they believe that message. For those who acknowledge they believe that message, we say things like, "Amen, you are in." In what? In the club, the Land of Born Again? Of course I believe that when a person accepts Jesus as their savior they are heaven bound when they die. The point I want to make is that Jesus preached the Gospel of the Kingdom.

That was His focus. If we are not careful, we are going to miss the entire point of what is available to us *here and now* in His Kingdom. One of Satan's favorite tactics in the Western Church is to keep us focused on heaven so that we are no earthly good to God here and now. The central message of Jesus is that He has established the Kingdom of God here on earth, and He wants it to continue to prosper through the life and ministry of every believer. Jesus preached the Kingdom of God, healed the sick and delivered those tied up in demonic oppression. All this is the supernatural. What's available to us is the supernatural lifestyle of the Kingdom. It is living your natural life aware of the benefits of the supernatural. It is sonship.

Once you change the way you think, everything changes. You are one thought away from walking in a level of power that you do not have to get with an encounter. It can come to you simply by changing the way you think. That is why the first words out of our Lord's mouth were urging us to change the way we think. He said that we are to enter through the narrow gate, for broad is the gate that leads to destruction and many enter through it. (See Matthew 7:13-14) Jesus is addressing Spirit-filled, believers. He is not talking about going through a narrow gate to heaven and a broad gate to hell. He is talking about a narrow gate to the top of the mountain as we ascend the mountain of God, to that place of deep friendship with Him where His expectations on you change. (See Psalm 24:3) The higher you go with God, the less wiggle room you have for stepping into obedient sin, or disobedient sin. What you can have is all of Him, but He now wants all of you. The narrow gate gives you access to the road that leads to life, *zoe*, Jesus, eternal life, relationship with the Father, power, protection, Psalm 91 and 92. Understand though, that access to the fullness of the Kingdom of God will squeeze the self-life right out of you. The narrow gate is not a promise of no conflict. Jesus walked so closely with the Father every day that He continually bumped up against the enemy. I want the same thing. If I am not bumping into the enemy, it is an indication that I am not on the narrow road.

The enemy's strategy for the church in the West is boredom and apathy. Those two things exist in the Land of Born Again, where all you hear Sunday after Sunday is, "Okay brothers and sisters, have you said yes to Jesus?" I am not talking about a message where I said yes to Jesus to become righteous. What I am talking about is that when I say yes to Jesus, I have no more rights. I am His *doulos*, His love slave. I am laid down. I have no opinions. He can do with me as He pleases. It is a place of surrender, of willfully choosing the narrow path. The broad path is destructive because it is filled with misconceptions and excuses. You can fail to recognize who you are and stay a spiritual orphan, or you can become so filled with pride you fail to recognize your dependence on the King and His sovereignty.

In a kingdom there is a King. Over 7,000 times in the Word, God is described as Lord, which means Master and Sovereign Ruler. Jesus can be your hombre buddy in the Born Again Land. In the Kingdom He is not your buddy. He is your Sovereign Master and mine, and I have never heard Him ask for my opinion on anything. In His Kingdom, you are in the King's domain. Psalm 24:1-2 says, "The earth is the LORD's, and everything in it, the world, and all who live in it; for He founded it on the seas and established it on the waters." The earth is His place of dominion. He is the Master. He is the Owner. It is *His* responsibility to take care of the people in *His* territory. It is *His* duty to protect *His* people, *His* duty to provide. Every part of the Kingdom is under the King's authority. You don't ever pursue suffering, or persecution, or walk into the teeth of the dog because you are looking for a fight. If you pursue Jesus on the narrow road, don't be surprised that the closer you get to Him the more you will begin to experience the things on this earth that He experienced. Many shy away from the narrow gate because it means total surrender. Total surrender means things like your checkbook are no longer your checkbook. If you do not sow your firstfruits into the church that you call home, you are not on the narrow road. You are still the owner of your resources. If you are easily offended all the time, you are not on the narrow road. If you are begrudgingly following Him, saying, "Well, I don't want to go to hell, and since there is no other way, then if this is what you want me to do, well then I guess I will," you are not on the narrow road. The narrow road that leads to life, is "You are the only One I want. You are the only One I need. I am loose change in your pocket. Keep me here or send me to some country I have never heard of, I don't care anymore. This is not my home." My quiet time is not snuggle time with my little buddy, Jesus. My quiet time is, "Jesus I am yours, whatever you want."

The wide road is where apathy burns. The narrow road is where passion burns. Many enter through the wide gate because it is easy. On the wide road you don't know who you are, don't know why you are here, don't know what you are doing. On the narrow road, you know who you are, you know who He is, and you are not hiding from the enemy. As a matter of fact, you are telling the Father, "Let the enemy know where I am at all times." On the wide road you beg God to please not let the devil hurt you. It is like that demonic prayer many pray over their kids at night—"Now I lay me down to sleep, if I should die before I wake." That's not the way of the Kingdom. Have we read James lately? You resist the devil and he will flee from you, he will run in stark terror from you. *You.* The narrow road is where courage comes upon you that others don't understand. When you are aware that you are under the King's domain, then you find rest. Rest gives you the courage to move, to act, not react. Don't be drawn to the charismatic out of fear of the devil. Books and tactics and strategies and prayers only take us so far. When we start praying prayers of gratitude, simply thanking Him, and agreeing with His plans, the enemy flees. Our prayers don't have to be complex. A simple "enemy stop" carries the full power of God. On the narrow road, we have fewer words and walk in greater power. On the narrow road, the Lord is the loudest voice in the room, the loudest voice in your narrative. On the narrow road, you say, "Most of all, Father, all I want is to walk in obedience. I don't even care about clarity for my future. I just want for today, to be at your feet, laid down."

The closer Jesus got to the cross, the fewer disciples He had. There was one disciple with Him at the cross and it was the youngest, the one who had his head on the chest of Jesus at the last supper. John had built such intimacy with Jesus that even when the others did not remain with Him, John did. John was willing to go through the narrow gate to get to the cross. Jesus looked at Peter and said, "Can you not just stay awake one night and pray for me? One night?" The narrow gate is the Father, Himself, and you have been invited in. You were chosen to be at His Table.

The further you ascend the mountain of God, the fewer will go with you. In a Holy Place, more light shines. And the more the light shines, the more the imperfections show. You would think that the closer you get to Father, Jesus and Holy Spirit, you would just celebrate who you are. Actually the closer you get, the more humble you become. When you get to the high place on the mountain, you glorify Him more and more. You actually celebrate your own weakness. People who are prideful never think they are prideful. When we fall, we never think we are falling. The way you keep from falling, is you stay low, you stay humble, you stay close to His chest. You recognize your need. You recognize that your need is for Him, the King, the Sovereign Master. Your humility and courage is what takes you to the top of the mountain on that ever so narrow road. You own nothing. The Apostle Paul got to the place when he said that he had learned to be content in all circumstances. He had learned that all that matters is to be with Elohim. "It is not I who live but Christ in me." (See Galatians 2:20) Paul's influence came through his own humility. He ascended the mountain by continually reminding himself of who he was not. Humility is not self-deprecation. Godly humility is recognizing the greatness of your King, and that with Him you can do more than you could ever imagine.

Even if you are 100 years old, the most powerful thought you can have is, "He is great." The only reason I am as clean as Jesus, the only reason

I can walk in power, the only reason I can pray and be prophetic, see signs, wonders, and healings, has nothing to do with me. This is just truth. 7,000 times in Scripture, He calls Himself "Master." The church of the West has lost this message. When we grow in our identities, we can begin to see that our own greatness is because of His; it is totally dependent on Him. Lucy in C.S. Lewis' book, *The Chronicles of Narnia: The Lion, the Witch, and the Wardrobe*, said it best when she said, "He is good, but He is not safe." He will call you to go where you have to rely on Him. It will take courage, but you can trust that He is good.

HEAR HIM ROAR

When was the last time you thanked Him just because you have breath in your lungs? When is the last time you looked over your business and thought, "I don't deserve any of this. It is all because of you. Thank you that I get to do this." Our view of God needs to be as huge as He is. The ultimate form of spiritual warfare is telling Him how big He is. If you walk the narrow road with gratitude and an awareness of the greatness of our Lord, then heaven will blow its wind on you all the days of your life. I look at my three children and my wife and I think, what have I done to deserve this? God is showing me to "Just stay there, don't take credit for any breakthrough." Exodus 34 says He is a jealous God. We should be burning for Him. When you give Him glory, He stands up with those huge wings in Revelation and the enemy nearly has a nervous breakdown. Spiritual warfare is not about hearing us roar. It's about hearing *Him* roar. He is a lion. Let Him out of the cage in your life. Pull a Jehoshaphat and let Him fight your battles.

If you want to take your battles into your own hands, the Father will let you and you will get annihilated. If your business is not doing well, perhaps it has nothing to do with natural realm economy. Perhaps it is tied to heaven's economy, where the least are the greatest. In the Kingdom, you have benefits that people in the Land of Born Again don't have. You have a different economy, a different health plan, a different business plan, and a different retirement plan. On the narrow road you have the wisdom of heaven available to you and the rights of a son. On the narrow road you do not have needs. This is why the Lord was so sad for the rich young ruler. All the Lord needed from him was everything. If the rich young ruler had given Him everything, He would have been given back even more. Ignorance is bliss in the Land of Born Again. Once you have revelation knowledge on the Kingdom, and you start to ascend the mountain, He requires one thing—to go higher you have to travel with less. This is why He sent the disciples into the various cities and told them to heal the sick, cleanse the lepers, and take nothing with them. (See Matthew 10:8) On the narrow road, you can't have anything with you. You become so integrated with Him, so relational, so confident in His love and wisdom that you can release the controls. You realize you are not flying the helicopter. You begin to trust more. We need to learn to be dependent on the One who has the plan, and knows how to make it happen. We need to learn to trust His timeline.

Some people pride themselves on having a detailed 7-year plan for their life. Be careful, because in the Kingdom we are told not to worry about tomorrow for tomorrow has enough worries of its own. So some of you are thinking, does this mean we are not to plan? That is not what I am saying. I am saying plan on His terms. Instead of asking for anointings and dreams for your life, ask, "Father, what is your dream for my life?" The reason people don't like this message of the Kingdom is because it doesn't cost you something, it costs you everything. There is nothing better than to be in a place where a job does not own you, money doesn't own you, where you only have one Owner, the Lord. My bills aren't my bills. My children's future is not up to me. It is a high level of trust to say, "I no longer have any wants." In the Land of Born Again, you have to figure out what you are going to do with your life. If you are constantly searching for clarity, searching and praying, asking God what is His will for your life, you won't find the answer until you surrender. When you surrender, the question of God's will for your life becomes irrelevant. He becomes your Master and you simply follow Him. "Whatever you do, work at it with all your heart, as working for the Lord, and not for human masters" (Colossians 3:23).

The Lord is your boss, He is your CEO, He is your provider, He is your dreamer, He is everything. A lot of people allow their jobs to become their King, their ruler, their sovereign. The Father is getting you to that narrow gate where you realize that a job is not your lord. It is amazing what happens when you open your hands and release control. Everything shifts. When you hang on to a little bit, heaven freezes over you. God is inviting you to live an open-handed life. The enemy tries to convince us that when we open our hands, it will go poorly. When you open yourself to God, He can't help Himself, He blesses you with more. If we are honest, many of us would never admit to being self-made people, but deep inside we actually do think we have a lot to do with our own success.

Choose the narrow road and the enemy runs from you. Choose the wide road and he will eat your lunch and pop the bag in your face. The narrow road is surrender; it is open hands and an open heart. It is, "Here I am." It is a simple prayer, with few words, yet it releases so much power. The power of the Most High guards you when you choose to stay in the place of abiding, resting on His chest, trusting beyond your own comprehension. Everyone benefits in the Kingdom when there is unity and trust—agreement with His will. You fall in, you take your position and accept His.

THE ROYAL FAMILY OF GOD

Jesus grew in wisdom and revelation. Take a moment to let that sink in. *Jesus grew.*

Revelation is when Kingdom truths just "get in you," when God opens your eyes to Truth. It is better than honey. Your body can age and fall apart, but you get revelation on this and inwardly you feel like Superman, or Wonder Woman. I would rather have revelation than encounters. Many people with encounters do not walk in integrity. They fall to the wayside because their trust is in the experience, in the encounter instead of in Him. Their pursuit is not deep friendship with Father. Their pursuit is to find another experience. I want revelation more than encounters. Revelation requires more faith. An encounter touches your senses. If you live from your senses, the enemy will take you out 10 times out of 9. Trust comes from experience and story. It is testimony. Trust is earned; it is different from love. We do not earn love. You are loved because you are in the family. The great testimonies of the Bible yield story after story of our Father's character. Maybe this is where we need to start. Start with the Word, and as you read it tell yourself, "This is mine. If You, Father, promised Noah a covenant then I am a part of that. You made a covenant with Abraham, and I am a part of that covenant." This kind of family has benefits, and the promises made to one are the promises made to all. If Jesus can do Father's works, then I can too. Build your own stories, but understand, your surrender will come at a cost. It will cost you your independence. Surrender is where you will find your greatest freedom.

Jesus lived a life of power because of His dependency. He studied the Word, He used the Word to bring truth to situations. Jesus came to bring light to the law, and the ways of Father. In His own humility He called His miracles His "Father's works." He was surrendered. He showed us how to live as family, within the Kingdom, in the King's domain. In the garden, as he sweated blood, He prayed. Three times He asked that the cup be taken from Him, and each time He surrendered. He said He only did what He saw the Father do, and only said what He heard the Father say. He spent hours each day in the Presence of Father, and then moved out to show a living example to the world and bring the Kingdom of heaven here to earth. Jesus showed us a simple way to live that was not safe, but it was good.

Growing in sonship means you outgrow the need to be independent. Do you remember what it was like to be 20? You thought you knew everything. No one could tell you anything, because you knew your methods would prove to be the best. Mama Jane called it being too big for your britches. You could not wait for all of the firsts: the first time you drove, the first date, the first car, the first time you lived away from your family, your wedding day, your first job, your first child, your first home. We are wired to leave the nest and go find our own adventures. In the Western Hemisphere, we are strongly independent. We are a democracy. America was birthed by people fighting for independence. "Let me vote. Listen to me. My opinion is right." We believe we can make our own way and be our own success story. It is very hard for us to release our will and say to Father, "Thy will be done, on earth as in heaven." It is hard because we do not understand the ways of Kingdom. We want to make our own way. Our greatest freedom is found the day we can raise our white flag and surrender.

As you grow in sonship and in recognizing you have a King, the benefits of Kingdom living become reality. You do not own your business, the King does. You do not possess your kids, they are the King's. Once you know who you are, you begin to see others in a new way. You are not competing for His attention, you have it. You are not fighting to be loved, you are loved. You are not pushing to get ahead of others because you recognize their worth and value too. You start to see through His eyes. His eyes of love and compassion. His eyes of power and strength.

Learning to abide, learning to rest, learning to be content as Paul says, is ongoing. It truly is as simple as believing God and trusting Him. Let Him be King. Let Him be found trustworthy. Face your fear of needing no one. Face the fact that you really do want to remain at the Table and are willing to give up control in order to find the most freedom. Most people think you have more freedom being independent. Think about it.

The truth will set you free. Who is the way, the truth and life? Who gives life abundantly? Why are you fighting to be free, when there is so much freedom in being the royal family of God?

Chapter 7

VULNERABILITY

I MET MY WIFE WENDY at the University of Georgia during the 1994 school year. The first night we went out together with a group of friends, I knew something was special about her. She was different in a good kind of way. It was obvious that she took her relationship with Jesus very seriously. She was funny, witty, and beautiful. At that point in my life, I was not in a good place. I had put on a lot of weight. My only interests as a 21-year-old were watching football, playing video games, and eating multiple boxes of Chef Boyardee on a daily basis. But suddenly, it was time to dream big.

For six months, I spent time with Wendy as a friend. She dated some of my friends, and I dated Papa John's pizza. She went out on dates and would come over to my house to talk about the Lord, what was going on in her life, and anything else that college kids talk about. I started noticing that these sessions were increasing rapidly. My lightning-fast mind finally figured something out: I had the chance of a lifetime and I was completely blowing it.

One night Wendy left my house around 3 a.m. after another long session of talking through life's difficulties and challenges. After she left, I told my college roommate, "You are looking at the Man in the Mirror. Michael Jackson sang it and I am about to live it. I'm about to make a change." Desperate times call for desperate measures. The next morning, I woke up and headed to Kmart to buy the unthinkable—a treadmill. Fatty was about to shock the world. I looked in the mirror that morning and said, "It's time for you to pay the piper, Pony Boy. No more fat college junior. The woman of your dreams is in your hands and you are going to lose her if you don't lose your gut." I got the treadmill and an infomercial special called the Gutbuster and started to lose some pounds. Things were changing. I went from wearing sweatpants, orange boots, and a lasagna-laced sweatshirt to khakis, Polo shirts, and nice shoes. My roommate thought I had gone mad, but I knew I was on the right path.

I could sense that Wendy knew something was up. Normally I smelled like a Philly cheesesteak, but now I smelled like the men's department at Macy's. The weight was coming off, and my inner James Bond was emerging. I was about to be the man of my best friend's dreams. At least, that's how it was playing out in my mind. The turning point was only a few days ahead. Visions of Casanova danced around in my mind as I formed my plan. I would woo this incredible woman of God and convince her to hop into my gladiator chariot and head off onto an expedition of changing the world for God—or something like that. Here was my plan:

invite Wendy over for a spaghetti dinner (spaghetti dinners are always more romantic). Kick my roommate out for the night. Turn on some Boyz II Men slow music. Kiss her. This was the plan, and I was going to execute it to perfection. That was, until the big night actually happened. Things like this never quite go down like you planned.

When Wendy got to my apartment, she looked at me like something was wrong. She could not figure out why the place was so clean. My apartment had not been cleaned in at least a year. On this night, however, it was apparent that something very important was about to go down. Wendy asked, "Why are you so dressed up? Are you OK?" I decided this was my moment that would reshape my story, so I went for it. I replied, "Before you leave here tonight, I'm going to kiss you." Webster defines the word awkward as, "causing difficulty, hard to deal with, causing or feeling embarrassment or inconvenience." I define awkward as that moment. Calling it awkward is actually the biggest understatement of my life. It was more awkward than a pregnant pole vaulter as Wendy and I stared at each other.

Wendy started laughing and said, "Are you kidding or being serious?" I said, "I'm being dead serious. It's going down." When we get to heaven, I'm going to ask God for a top 10 most awkward list of first kisses between couples who ended up getting married. I'll bet you a hundred bucks Wendy and I are on the list. The kiss lasted about fifteen seconds, and she left. I sat on my couch and thought, "What just happened?" When she got home, she called me, and we both agreed that it was stranger than a Tim Burton movie. Twenty years later, I still laugh about our awkward start. We have three kids, a mortgage, and a natural gas bill. Things worked out to say the least. We've been in active ministry from the very beginning of our marriage and now we pastor Bridgeway Church. Over the years we've had some ups and downs, just like any other married couple. Six years ago, we had our biggest down yet when we hit the first crisis in our marriage. I had no idea God would use it to lead us to a greater understanding of how grace produces literal transformation. It happens not only in marriages, but also in the Supernatural when we pray for people, because grace flows through vulnerability. And vulnerability marks our lives when we're locked in at the Table. Before I tell you our story, I want to look at a famous passage in the Bible—the story of Zacchaeus.

METANOIA – BE TRANSFORMED BY THE RENEWING OF YOUR MIND.

> *Jesus entered Jericho and was passing through. A man was there by the name of Zacchaeus; he was a chief tax collector and was wealthy. He wanted to see who Jesus was, but because he was short he could not see over the crowd. So he ran ahead and climbed a sycamore-fig tree to see him, since Jesus was coming that way. When Jesus reached the spot, he looked up and said to him, "Zacchaeus, come down immediately. I must stay at your house today." So he came down at once and welcomed him gladly. All the people saw this and began to mutter, "He has gone to be the guest of a sinner." But Zacchaeus stood up and said to the Lord, "Look, Lord! Here and now I give half of my possessions to the poor, and if I have cheated anybody out of anything, I will pay back four times the amount." Jesus said to him, "Today salvation has come to this house, because this man, too, is a son of Abraham. For the Son of Man came to seek and to save the lost."*
>
> *Luke 19:1-10*

I've always been drawn to real people. I have a very difficult time being around pretentious people. I think it's because I know how much of a train wreck I am on a daily basis without Jesus. We are all broken and in need of a Savior. That's why I resonate with people like Zacchaeus more than I do the religious, upright, and arrogant. When God showed me how many principles in this passage literally lead to seeing people healed,

I was amazed. I believe that the reason we do not see more healings as we minister is because we don't think like Jesus. When we start thinking like Jesus, we will see what He sees. God is not holding out on us—He is waiting on us to line up our minds with His reality. He is waiting for us to lay aside all our Lo-debar thinking and live at the King's Table. Unless we transform our minds to the key principles of Scripture, we will go a lifetime and never feast at the King's Table, never taste the Kingdom of God and its power.

When I was younger, I had a hard time reading the Bible. Even though I loved Jesus very much, I could not find the passion to devour His Word. I finally realized in one season of my life that I had grown up with the mentality that the primary purpose of Jesus was to get me into heaven when I died. That mentality—that misconception—worked against me in many ways. I had no revelation that Jesus actually died to reconnect me with the Father. I was completely and utterly shocked to discover that Jesus and His Word were actually an invitation to the King's Table where I can build the deep friendship with Father that He intended from the beginning. When I fully started to believe this, I started to notice principles in the Bible that helped me *metanoia*—transform my mind. The more I allowed God's Word to transform my mind, the more the supernatural realm took on a greater reality than the natural. As that transformation took hold, I began to see more healings manifest when I prayed for people. It's one thing to think about God. It's an entirely new thing to begin to believe that you can actually think *like* God. Once we start thinking like God, we begin to see what God sees. Breakthrough is a natural outflow of this process. With that in mind, we can see that the story of Zacchaeus has powerful implications.

Zacchaeus' story is the perfect dance of what I call the "Ephesians 2:8 Two-Step," which states, "For it is by grace you have been saved, through faith—and this is not from yourselves, it is the gift from God." So often we don't see God's power manifest as we minister because we are thinking like orphans. Orphans are not totally convinced that God wants to move on their behalf. When we're living in Lo-debar, we don't yet understand His will, nor do we know what our role is in partnering with Him. We do not know how to dance with grace. When God showed me how to start dancing with Him, I began seeing healings—lots of them. At Bridgeway Church, we are always asking God to show us how to dance with grace. Zacchaeus' story shows us how the dance of grace works. What is so interesting to me about his story is that grace transformed him so quickly that he offered to pay back a lot of money he had embezzled. Jesus did not command him to do that. God's grace impacted Zacchaeus so much that it did not take a command from God for him to respond with grace. Zacchaeus' vulnerability led to a grace invasion that led to transformation. Vulnerability matters in our ability to stay pulled up tight to the Table and in the arena of breakthrough. As a matter of fact, it is the recipe for breakthrough. The reason we do not see more breakthrough in our ministries and in our own lives is that we focus on having huge faith. Jesus said that all we need is mustard seed faith. We don't have faith problems. We have love and vulnerability problems that come from Lo-debar mindsets. That is what's keeping us from breakthrough.

I have been obsessed with the idea of knowing God most of my life. *Really* knowing Him. I've wanted and still want a true and authentic relationship with Him. At the same time, even the thought of God can be completely overwhelming. I'm sure you've felt that way too. A few years ago a friend of mine told me I needed to listen to a TED talk by Brené Brown. Since I'm really trendy, my response was, "What's a TED talk?" I Googled it and found out that TED stands for technology, entertainment, and design, and TED talks are short presentations—18 minutes long—given at TED conferences. These talks can be on any subject, as long as they have a relevant message for a wide global audience. TED wants to deliver engaging speakers whose presentations discuss new concepts and are supported by evidence. So, with the help of my friend, I stumbled upon Brené Brown's TED talk. I'm sure glad I did. Brené is a professor at the University of Houston Graduate College of Social Work. She has written two different New York Times® bestsellers: *Daring Greatly* and *The Gifts of Imperfection*. The TED talk that my friend recommended to me has become one of the five most popular TED talks of all time. It is titled, "The Power of Vulnerability."[1] I had no idea that God was setting me up, and using a TED talk to do it. Brené's thoughts on vulnerability instigated a radical shift in my heart and mind. As I listened, I knew what she was sharing had dramatic implications in the Kingdom of God. I won't repeat her entire talk for you. I urge you to listen for yourself.

As I listened, a dam broke free inside of me when I realized that down deep in my core it's not possible to have intimacy with God without a high level of vulnerability. Lo-debar thinking always keeps your guard up—it works against vulnerability. At the King's Table, sons and daughters just want to sit next to Papa. We want to be near Him no matter what anybody thinks, and that passion gives us the confidence to be vulnerable. As we grow in vulnerability, His power to impact others for the Kingdom seems to "accidentally" increase in us. I started to see a pattern: vulnerability leads to intimacy with God and others, which leads to a higher level of power in both of those relationships. Where there is no vulnerability, there is no power. It sounds so simple, but the implications are enormous. I started to ask the question: "Is it possible that God is not looking for people to become charismatic—He's simply looking for people to become vulnerable?" As I began to change my thinking and dared to be vulnerable, I also noticed a dramatic increase in the prophetic in my life and ministry.

Vulnerability is the state of being exposed. This realization led me to ask myself a lot of questions about whether I lived my life in a plastic

---

1. https://www.ted.com/talks/brene_brown_on_vulnerability

state or if was I truly becoming a person who did not feel the need to guard myself as if everything was always OK with me. As I asked from the perspective of my relationship with God and with other people, I started to notice that some key characters in the Bible showed more vulnerability than I did—and that I could learn from them.

DANCING WITH GRACE

Zacchaeus and another Bible character, the woman with the issue of blood, have a lot in common. Both of them knew Jesus was on the scene. Think about this for a moment. Jesus was on the scene for many other people besides Zacchaeus and the woman with the issue of blood, but they received something the others did not. I think they received because they knew how to dance with grace. This woman pulled an Ephesians 2:8 and exercised her faith in Jesus. To her, grace was a person, not a concept. The moment I stopped seeing grace as a subject to be studied, and started seeing grace as a person to be embraced, healings began to manifest. Believing in Jesus but remaining in Lo-debar means practically nothing in the supernatural realm. Even demons believe in Jesus. Believing in Jesus is not enough. Pulling yourself up to the Table, having faith in the grace He offers, and knowing how to receive this grace, are incredibly important.

Matthew 9:20-22 shows us that this woman displayed enough vulnerability to receive healing from grace itself. As I've studied healing over the last 15 years, time and time again I've noticed the connection between the faith and the breakthrough. Yet, it wasn't until that short TED talk that God began to show me there is even more in play—that vulnerability is the key. When a person is not guarded, when he or she is willing to lay fears aside and become emotionally exposed, it has an undeniable effect on breakthrough. Perhaps our need for enormous faith is overrated. Maybe it's more important to have courageous vulnerability.

I love what Paul says in Romans 7:15-25:

> *I do not understand what I do. For what I want to do I do not do, but what I hate I do. And if I do what I do not want to do, I agree that the law is good. As it is, it is no longer I myself who do it, but it is sin living in me. For I know that good itself does not dwell in me, that is, in my sinful nature. For I have the desire to do what is good, but I cannot carry it out. For I do not do the good I want to do, but the evil I do not want to do - this I keep on doing. Now if I do what I do not want to do, it is no longer I who do it, but it is sin living in me that does it. So I find this law at work: Although I want to do good, evil is right there with me. For in my inner being I delight in God's law; but I see another law at work in me, waging war against the law of my mind and making me a prisoner of the law of sin at work within me. What a wretched man I am! Who will rescue me from this body that is subject to death? Thanks be to God, who delivers me through Jesus Christ our Lord! So then, I myself in my mind am a slave to God's law, but in my sinful nature a slave to the law of sin.*

Paul is talking about pride. Perhaps one reason so many of us still live in Lo-debar and don't see more healings is not because of our healing theology, but because of pride. Pride and vulnerability oppose each other. Paul accomplished so much in his life, yet he was incredibly vulnerable. He boasted in something other than himself; he boasted in his weakness. "If I must boast, I will boast of the things that show my weakness" (2 Corinthians 11:30). To walk in the power Paul walked in, we must be willing to study and embrace the humility and vulnerability he walked in. There is no way around it. Even Jesus said, "Don't you believe that I am in the Father, and that the Father is in me? The words I say to you I do not speak on my own authority. Rather, it is the Father, living in me, who is doing his work" (John 14:10). Humility and vulnerability go hand in hand. So many people have been turned off by the idea of entertaining anything, like healing, that they miss how being charismatic should not be the goal. Vulnerability should be the goal. I believe that if a new breed of vulnerable Christians rises, we will see all the gifts of the Holy Spirit manifest as we learn to think and posture our hearts and minds differently—as sons and daughters at the King's Table instead spiritual orphans in Lo-debar.

Zacchaeus and the woman with the issue of blood were willing to lower themselves in a posture of humility, creating banks for God's river of grace to flow. Zacchaeus humiliated himself by climbing up a tree to be able to see Jesus. The woman with the issue of blood crawled on her hands and knees to get to grace. The old saying "it's all about grace" isn't exactly right. It's all about learning how to dance with grace. Grace does not transform me until I come to the end of myself, lay aside my orphan mindset, and admit that I need it. Grace is available to all, but only a few experience it. The two men who cried "Have mercy on us, Son of David!" (See Matthew 9:27-31) show us how to dance with grace. They showed vulnerability by following Jesus and admitting their own inadequacies. Grace can be available to a proud man and never affect him. But the moment he says, "God, help me, I can't fix myself," we see healing. Vulnerability is like a suction cup for the miraculous of God. As sons and daughters, we can embrace vulnerability because we can trust that grace will be our landing pad. If we're truly convinced that we are dependent on the Father for everything, then being vulnerable with Him and others follows naturally.

AT THE FOOT OF THE FIG TREE

God undeniably put my wife and me together. We both knew it soon after that first awkward kiss. As we started dating, we began heading toward a lifetime of pursuing God and serving Him together. When you are young and in love, as we were, you have zero concept of what awaits you on the other side of "I do." The other side is a daily reminder that you are not the most important person in the world, and that the goal of marriage is to out-give, out-forgive, and out-serve the other person. Little did either of us know in the moments after that awkward first kiss how hard it would be to learn selflessness and discover what taking up our cross in our marriage actually looks like.

I have heard about the 3, 7, or 15-year itch to move on from marriage. I have no idea if any of these numbers are true, but it's interesting how many times I hear this as I pastor people. I just never thought I would be itchy. I never thought in a million years that divorce would be an option for Wendy and me. When I said "I do," I meant it. I am a loyal person by nature, and I hadn't had a single thought of our marriage not lasting before "it" hit. "It" was another dark night of the soul, another season that literally stretched our faith to the brink of giving up. Our marriage hit this place, and neither one of us saw it coming. There were no affairs, pornography addictions, financial crises, or any other major event that tears so many marriages apart. We simply got to the place where we could not be in the same room together very long without disagreeing or arguing about something. I remember sitting in my recliner one night and thinking, "There is a realistic chance of me going through what I never thought was an option." It was a scary place that left us both feeling hopeless. There appeared to be no resolution in sight to the continuous conflict. Life got scarier as the arguments become calmer, as if we had both resigned ourselves to the fact that it would never get better. When that kind of apathy sets in, the enemy goes to work.

One night, I walked outside and took a baseball bat to my trash can. I pounded on that trash can as I wept. I've heard it said many times that our biggest breakthroughs come after our biggest breakdowns. In that moment, I highly doubted it. If you had asked either one of us about the cause of this inability to get along, I'm not sure we would have been able to articulate it. There is no telling how much warfare we go through as we give our lives to Jesus and His Kingdom. All we knew is that we needed help. We had reached the point in life where we knew we had better do something drastic or things would never change. We had to risk vulnerability in order to see change. For Zacchaeus, that moment came at the foot of a fig tree. Our fig tree was in Buena Vista, Colorado, at Crossroads Christian Counseling. As pastors, we knew it was risky to let our guard down and admit we needed help. After I weighed the cost, I decided I did not care what others thought. We needed help, and it was time to let our guards down. Without vulnerability, there was little chance of breakthrough for us.

My wife and I sat down and talked one night about the reality of our situation. There was no yelling or hatred. We were both simply scared, fragile, and numb. Wendy and I are both passionate people who fully engage the things we are passionate about. Numb is not a word to describe either of us. But on this night, it was the perfect description. As our kids slept upstairs, we discussed the magnitude of our conflict. We decided to leave the next week for a week of therapy. We landed in Denver and drove up the interstate through a truly spectacular view. On this three-hour drive, I felt like we were in a scene from *The Lord of the Rings*. I wasn't able to stop staring at the beauty of the mountains. I had no idea that this three-hour drive would begin a three-year journey of discovering what love really is. I did not realize what God was planning for our marriage. I wish I knew then what I know now—that this trip was only the first of two major, life-changing weeks for us.

Our first week in Colorado with a therapist was enlightening, intense, refreshing, and challenging. It centered on the idea of changing thought patterns and behaviors. It's interesting how the most powerful truths always make their way back to the root of who Jesus was and what He taught. Earlier in this book, I pointed out that Jesus began His ministry with, "Repent, for the kingdom of heaven has come near" (Matthew 4:17). This idea of repentance is all about *metanoia*—the concept of changing thought patterns. That's what Colorado was for our marriage.

God challenged us gently to change the way we thought about each other and about what love was in the first place. We knew quickly in counseling that God was bringing us closer together, but we did not realize how hard it is to change thinking patterns so that they lead to transformation. It would take us three years to truly see transformational breakthrough. I am convinced, beyond a shadow of a doubt, that two things are against most people when it comes to successfully staying at the King's Table and seeing a culture of the supernatural manifest in their families and their churches. The first is an unwillingness to be vulnerable enough to see grace explode, and the second is an unwillingness to be patient enough to be astonished.

During the three years between our two trips to Colorado, we saw some improvement, off and on, in our marriage. Like most people, we took a couple of steps forward and then a few steps back. This cycle was not all bad. There were times we truly knew God was at work. The work He was doing reached a crescendo on our second trip. I can honestly say it was the deepest and most impactful week of spiritual formation I've ever had in 45 years on this big beautiful planet.

I want to stay at the King's Table and sit as close to my Papa as possible. I want to continue to see miracles and healings. It never gets old to me. I love seeing the power of God manifest when I pray for people. I love the fact that I pastor a church that is going after the supernatural in a very natural way. We have testimonies on a weekly basis of people seeing healings in their lives. When God restores real and genuine physical ailments, we celebrate it at Bridgeway Church. Yet, even with the command of Jesus to heal the sick, and my passion to do so, there is something much greater that I have learned and experienced—and it happened in my own marriage.

A LOVE REVELATION

On our second trip to counseling in Colorado, we both thought we were going for a tune-up. We were wrong. Jesus had something greater in store for us. In our second and third sessions, we came to a point where we were simply not getting along very well. We both discussed what our own needs were for each other with the help of our therapist. Midweek, I decided to go for a workout at a CrossFit gym. At the end of my workout, out of the blue, I looked up to heaven and said, "What's the point down here? What do you want from me?" Immediately I heard, "Greater love has no one than this: to lay down one's life for one's friends" (John 15:13). He spoke to me so clearly that it was like He was standing right beside me. I immediately got into my car and said to the Lord, "I know what love is. I just want you to show me what it is. Make it personal. I know what it is, but what is it really?" The next song that immediately came on my XM radio was one I had not heard in a long time. It was Foreigner's "I Want to Know What Love Is." The Lord has a sense of humor.

I've had the Lord tell me many things before, in my walk with Him. I've had some wild and out-of-the-box experiences with Him. I've seen blind eyes open, a gold glory cloud manifest in a church service, food multiply, and a demon-possessed lady in Haiti dramatically delivered. I have had words of knowledge over people that I could not possibly have known. I have had dreams and revelation from heaven. I have had strategic plans come to me that are beyond my ability to create. But I'll tell you right now that none of those things can hold a fork to the powerful word spoken to me by the Word Himself in this moment. I understood love on a different level. He said, "Maybe you don't have a faith problem. Maybe you simply have a love problem." I have learned to recognize the difference between knowledge and revelation. What God spoke to me was pure revelation. My response was, "OK, I get it." The next two days in counseling felt like Jesus Christ had walked into our sessions. We got more revelation on love in two days than we had in 18 years of marriage. We realized on a gut level what being a safe place meant for each other. We also started to understand on a practical level what it looked like to love each other. Our postures began to change from "not receiving" to "giving." We genuinely began to ask what the other person needed on a daily basis. Even now with our Colorado experience behind us, we realize that this is a lifelong process of choosing to be vulnerable every single day in our marriage.

It has been a long journey for us to realize what being a safe person for each other looks like, and it has not been easy. It has taken a lot of vulnerability. The point is that our vulnerability gave grace a target to hit. We have seen grace truly transform us and the way we see each other. I'm not sure it is possible to build deep friendship with God without walking in vulnerability. Perhaps vulnerability is a little-talked about trait of someone who flows in a high level of the prophetic. Perhaps we have made God more charismatic than He is. Perhaps if we would learn a few key principles, that even people outside of Christ are discovering, then we would see naturally supernatural cultures manifest by accident. Our time together in Colorado was so powerful that we decided to renew our vows. The Lord worked it out perfectly. A married couple who really helped us to process all that God did there in Buena Vista performed the ceremony. The whole experience was impactful because it genuinely centered on the idea of what love really is—sacrificial, giving, non-judging, powerful love.

I am convinced that we will see more supernatural power manifest in our ministries when we embrace vulnerability and love instead of focusing most of our attention on faith. Many people who begin to see healing manifest in their lives and ministries get sidetracked and pursue those things for the wrong reasons. What if, when we prayed for people, we genuinely and deeply listened and cared about the need at hand? What if we loved? Think what it could be like if we had the courage to let vulnerability lead us in the right direction. We could lead powerful communities that walk in the works and the ways of Father, while at the same time being vulnerable about where we are in our own lives. We would see more breakthrough if we could learn to boast in our weakness and allow the grace of the most magnificent person who has ever existed to flow into the brokenness in our lives and the lives of others. It's about learning to love—not just loving Jesus, but loving one another too. I believe that if we could bring love into our families, our workplace, and our communities we would see God's transformational power flow abundantly.

Chapter 9

THE CULTURE OF
THE WORD

OUR SON JACK NORRIS got a new life jacket recently so our family could go on a trip to the lake. When he put it on, he looked at his mom and sister and said, "I am the golden child," as he strutted around in his bright yellow life jacket. Everyone laughed because not only does he believe that, his siblings will tell you that he is the golden child. I know what that feels like. I hope you do too. I hope there was someone in your life who treated you like you were the most special person in the world. It may have been a coach, a teacher, a Sunday School teacher, your boss, your parents, or your grandparents. Many of us understand love because we have experienced unconditional love. And there are many of us who are challenged when it comes to recognizing love because the people who should have loved us were broken, and love was conditional— it had markers you had to reach for approval. In the Kingdom, you are the golden child. For the rest of your life, you can continue to grow in that revelation. You can continue to grow in the knowledge that you are a golden child, and that you are blessed because you are loved unconditionally by the creator of the universe who is your Father.

STAYING ON THE NARROW ROAD

I love to create awkward moments and then watch how people respond. There are just some things you can say that guarantee a moment more awkward than a hairless cat. Some things simply trigger people on a deep level and cause them to be stunned into silence. In Christian circles, a conversation on prosperity will do this 10 times out of 9.

Prosperity. That word triggers the orphan spirit. What was your immediate response when you read that word just now? Talking about prosperity in the church brings out some pretty strong emotions in people. I'm not talking about this because I read someone's book. I'm talking about this because of Genesis 26 and the book of John. When you read the book of John, you realize that Jesus is really nice. He never made anyone sick, and He healed a lot of people. He talked about intimacy with the Father, over and over, then He healed people. Our healing ministry at Bridgeway didn't start with our own experiences, it started with reading the Word. We just kept reading the gospels over and over, and we started to believe what had been written, and that it was for today. We began by believing His Word—the Word that tells us our Jesus did not die on a cross so we can be miserable and just make it until we get to heaven. The Word promises us that we can do the same things as Jesus and even greater things, because we have the power of Holy Spirit with us. At Bridgeway we started to believe that we are loved and that His compassion brings freedom to others who are suffering.

When you build your life on the rock of His written Word, you don't have to be a parasite, always depending on what other people say or teach. You move from listening to the latest feel good podcast, to actually feeding yourself on the Word and the revelation it brings to you. You don't have to go to someone else to live off of their blood and off what the Father is showing them. I hear people say, "I just don't feel the love of God." Could it be because there's not enough Word operating in them? Read Mark 4:1–20. When the Word gets in you, when the Seed gets in you, when the Seed gets in *us*, the Seed begins to grow. At that point, Satan doesn't come to attack *you*, he comes to attack the Seed in you. Jesus basically said that if you do not understand this parable, you don't understand anything. The farmer scatters seed, then the power comes as the seed gets down in the soil.

When there's no power in my life, instead of going from place to place, conference to conference trying to find it, I need to stop and get into the Word so that the Word can get in me. I'm lacking because there is a lack of seed growing in me. It begins with the Seed of the Word.

If I am in a love deficit with the Father, turning to someone else to fill that deficit isn't going to do it. There is a better way. Take ten passages about His love and get the Seed down into you. Then, in community, let that seed be watered by other people's words falling on top of the written Word in you. Let the podcasts and conference speakers water what is already growing in you. Over time, you will find that you have fruit. You will begin to believe the Word. You will begin to shape your thoughts according to that Truth. You will have a new confidence, built not on faith, or circumstances, but on the very principles of the Word of God. You can have faith, and you can have faith for a misconception. This is why we need the Word and Spirit along with our community of believers to help us stay on the narrow road. You keep getting the Word in you until you reach the point when the Seed begins to take root and becomes so strong that you can't pull it up. I love a prophetic culture, but I don't love it more than a Word culture. It has happened again and again over the course of history—the Holy Spirit lands in a place and a movement is birthed with a strong foundation on the Word, but then it became about the Spirit. We need to understand that it is not either/or—Spirit or Word—it is Spirit *and* Word. The Spirit of God testifies to the Word of God.

I highly value the prophetic and I strive to grow in it every day, because according to 1 Corinthians 14, as I pursue love, a natural outcome is that I will want to love others, building and encouraging them through the prophetic gift of the Spirit. I value the gifts of the Spirit. But for those of us who call ourselves Christians, our invitation is to honor both the written Word of God and the prophetic word. We need both. Let us walk in a high level of supernatural ministry, doing Father's works, but also with a desire for expository preaching and systematic Bible study. I don't want to check my brain at the door. Jesus Christ had a PhD in the Torah *and* He walked on water. The world is starving for a movement where you actually do not check your brains at the door. Why can you not lay hands on the sick, see them recover, and still have a PhD beside your name? Just because I walk in things of the Spirit doesn't mean I have to scream at you. I don't have to act weird. There's power in the Word. Many times, when people are so crazy loud, it's an overcompensation for what's not inside of them. Get the Seed in you. Treat people with honor. Stop yelling. You can struggle in the prophetic as you navigate the naturally supernatural, but none of us should be struggling in the Word. A culture of freedom, a culture of honor, a prophetic culture where the Holy Spirit is moving—it all builds on the foundation of the Word. If we don't build everything, including the prosperity, abundance, and multiplication message, upon the Word, then we're just a bunch of people getting stirred up about nothing. It becomes about our own opinions, not His.

When the rubber meets the road and all hell invades your life, you're going to have to respond to hell the same way your King did. He responded out of His mouth with the written Word of God. You want to talk about the prophetic? There's never been anyone more prophetic than Jesus Christ, and He did not respond to the devil with a rhema Word. He quoted the logos. The New Testament is primarily written in two languages, Greek and Aramaic. There are two words that are used in the New Testament for the Word. One is *rhema*, which is the inspired or spoken Word. This is when Father speaks to you through visions, dreams, words of knowledge, words of wisdom, prophetic insight, thoughts, and other prophets. We hear this phrase often, "I just feel like the Lord is showing me." That's great. Rhema words are awesome. They help us to see that the God of the universe sees us, and that He is alive and working right now. The other word used in Scripture for the Word, is *logos*, referring to the written Word. Jesus is described as the Word made flesh. We see in Him the intentions of Father regarding how to live out the written Word. The Word of God was first given to the Israelites in the form of scrolls. They so honored the Word that it was kept in the Ark of the Covenant as they wandered through the desert. In another desert Jesus showed us that we now have access to the Word and we can unroll it for ourselves. We do not need a priest to interpret. The Word is ours now. It is ours to use to combat the enemy. A question to ask yourself in any circumstance you face is, "What does the Word say? What was written to me almost 2,000 years ago?" We cannot underestimate the importance of the Word. Heaven is released over you when, with your own mouth you speak the Word of God.

Ask for hunger, then just start reading your Bible. Just begin. If you fail, then get up and start again tomorrow. Keep at it. Write Post-it notes of Scripture and plaster them all over your walls, your bathroom mirror, your desk. Remind yourself of what is true. Be a student of the Word. Seeking first the Kingdom of God includes going to the Lord, your Master, your Sovereign King, in prayer and the counsel of the Word. Prophetic words are good, but the Word of God is our foundation. Seek God and He will answer you. He will show you the way.

HIS LAVISH ABUNDANCE

We have learned that Lo-debar is the land of barrenness, a place of lack, a place of bitterness. It's a difficult place to live. David was King, and he led Israel in 40 years of peace and abundance. When you are connected to the Father, the natural outcome is that His abundance floods you. We know the King's Table is where the spiritual son or daughter says, "I am not an orphan. I will not make excuses for what I do not have. I will not get offended." In previous chapters, we've talked about indicators that we're growing in sonship. Here's another one: getting out of all-or-nothing thinking. I'm not sure any of us ever fully understand what it is to live as a son. We have a hard time grasping what's offered to us by Calvary. Let's make the concept scalable. If we look to Jesus as our example of a Son, who lived at the 100% mark, we can see where we fall. When He was born, Herod tried to kill him. He had no place to lay His head. His number-one disciple could not even stay awake while He was praying in the garden. Jesus had everything you can imagine come against Him and it never deterred Him from His intimate connection with the Father. If that's 100%—where coins are showing up in fish's mouths—then 0% is Lo-debar thinking—"I never have anything. Nobody likes me. God hates me. He would never bless me." You are back in the land of lack, barrenness, and bitterness. This is one of the reasons we need the Word of God, the Spirit who is the Counselor, *and* community. We need our friends to tell us when we have moved away from truth, when we start to slide back down the scale. If you live isolated from others, always self-protecting, then the enemy can play with you like a cat does with a mouse.

Many believers walk in a high level of character and integrity, but when someone brings up money or prosperity or blessing, walls go up immediately. I believe this is because a lot of us grew up under a distorted paradigm where our theology was formed around the idea that He is "the God of just enough." There's a small problem with this. Yeshua, just a normal-looking rabbi, shows up in the New Testament and changes everything. His coming-out party, in John 2, was the first miracle in the New Testament. At the end of a wedding, when there was no more wine, He told them to go fill up six stone jars with water. Let this sink in for a second here because we are talking about over 700 bottles of wine. They obeyed, then He turned the water into wine. Plus, His wine tasted a million times better than anything the guests had ever tasted. Here's the question: Why would He need to provide that much wine at the end of the party? Why did He make it taste so delicious? Wouldn't that be wasteful? No, it wasn't wasteful. Jesus' coming-out party demonstrates that He is the "God of too much who likes abundance." His miracle did not fulfill a need, it was not a healing, it was not even a prophetic word or the issue of an assignment. His first miracle was filled with joy. It was an indication of abundance. When we go to heaven, some of us are going to be shocked that our houses are not busted up and sitting on nasty red clay. It is so immaculate in heaven, so pristine, it makes Augusta National look like a flea market in Gaffney, South Carolina.

I heard the Father say to me, "Many people will be very uncomfortable when they come up here to heaven." A lot of us would be more comfortable in a one-bedroom flat up there with Him than we would be letting Him lavish His abundance upon us. I truly believe that the highest form of pride is the inability to receive. I think an even higher level of pride is refusing to accept abundance from the One you say you love so much. I don't mean provision. I'm talking about abundance. There's a difference in provision and abundance. Some of us would go over to the huge jars of wine, stick just one pinky in, and say, "Oh God, you're so good." He would say, "Why are you just stinking your pinky in there, son? I made six barrels." Abundance.

It wasn't just those jars of wine. Peter witnessed Jesus provide an unbelievable abundance of fish when previously there were none. (See John 21:1– 6) Simon Peter, a professional fisherman, had fished all night and caught nothing. All of a sudden, the Lord said, "You caught anything?" (By the way, if the Father, Jesus, or Holy Spirit ever asks you a question, I guarantee you, they know the answer before they ask you. That's a fact.) Simon Peter confirmed he had caught no fish all night. Jesus told him to just throw the net out on the other side of the boat. When I imagine Simon Peter's response to the Lord, it looks like, "Bless your heart. We're professionals and we're telling you, there are no fish." Jesus told him to just throw the net out there. When he obeyed and threw it, the nets filled with fish. It says in the Greek that the nets began to tear. Abundance.

Why is this issue of abundance so important? It's important because it reveals Jesus' nature. When you know the nature of someone, you can predict their behavior. If you don't believe what's revealed about His character in Scripture, then you can be afforded rights your whole life and never experience them because you never align your thoughts to the thoughts of the Father. You never acknowledge just how nice He is, how good He is. I promise you—He is so good. I am constantly overwhelmed by His goodness.

BLESSINGS OVERFLOWING

Most of us believe that God can train us in the desert seasons, but has it ever occurred to you that He can train you through favor? You may say, "That doesn't fit my theology." Well, perhaps it's time to change your theology to match God's. The world doesn't revolve around the way you think or the way I think. The world revolves around the way He *is*. He was a blesser in the Garden to Adam and Eve. He blessed Abraham, Joseph, David, and Job—yes, even Job. What we need to do is take the stories of His goodness and believe that He loves to bless us, even now.

Jesus said, nineteen times, "Let it be done to you as you believe." I'm simply saying, let's get to the King's Table and let it be done to us as we believe, according to His written Word. I am not leaning on someone else's revelation on this. I have dug into the Scriptures for a long time searching out wisdom on abundance. I used to think God made people sick to get glory out of it. Then, 16 years ago, Father asked me if Jesus ever made anyone sick. I searched the Word and could not find anything that said He did, so I had to conclude that He didn't. I read the Scriptures and started believing what the Scripture said, and then? Then, I just happened to see healings manifest. I just happened to start praying in tongues. I just happened to start walking with the Holy Spirit in power. Then God asked me, "Will you let me do with you on abundance, what I did with everything else?" I said "Yes," and He proceeded to take my little Le Sueur pea-brain-thinking self, who loved Him with all my heart, and said, "Chad, if you will let Me, I'll get your Le Sueur-pea-thinking out of your brain and I'll give you My thoughts, because My thoughts are higher than your thoughts." My reply was, "If You'll show me, I'll do it."

I started looking up passages on abundance, prosperity, and provision from the Father, and what I found blew me away. He didn't just give a little bit. He didn't just meet people's needs. From the Scriptures—not from other people's stories—I began to realize that He's a way more generous giver than I ever thought He was. Then, that truth began showing up in my life. God told me to start ordering the most expensive meal on the menu when I went out on date nights with my wife. I tried to cast that demon out. The first time I obeyed, we went to a place with a menu I can't pronounce and I ordered the most expensive meal. Then, I got a surprise the next day. Someone at church came up and said, "The Father told me to bless you with this." The amount they gave me was at least 3 times the amount I paid for the meal.

How did God break me of my Le Sueur pea-thinking? He had me step into generosity and then generosity started to manifest itself back to me. The orphan spirit may well up and say, "Be careful with this message, because someone may go and buy some $900,000 car in the name of abundance." Hang on there and realize something—I didn't do anything the Father didn't tell me to do. The Father told me, "When you go on a date with your wife, do this." He did not tell me to go buy a Lamborghini. He didn't tell me to max out our credit cards. I only did what He told me to do. When I obeyed, He blessed us. In the midst of all this, I realized that my generosity matters too. Instead of giving out of obligation, I started giving out of a heart of love. It's undeniable what's happening not just in my finances, but also in my marriage, with my kids, with my friends, in this church, with my family and extended family. I have to ask, has it ever occurred to us that the message of abundance goes way beyond cash? Abundance is not just about money. God's message of abundance affects every area of life. We tend to look at finances because it is an easy indicator of our identity as a son or an orphan. I say all the time at Bridgeway, "Show me your checkbook and I will tell you what you value."

This orphan spirit scale is not mystical. What is the orphan spirit? It is a mindset that does not align to the message of royalty as presented in the gospels. I am a co-heir to Jesus. He's called me to be the head not the tail. He has called us to reign with Him. We think it honors God to walk in a high level of character and discipline. He does value this, but what really turns His stomach the wrong way is when we do those things, but our thinking is contrary to His on abundance. He wants to give abundance in all aspects of life; in relationships, generosity, healing, and in intimacy with Him. *All* is available to us. The shift comes when we realize He is the owner. If He says, "Be generous," then be generous. Orphans hold on for fear of never having enough. Sons realize that there is more than enough.

Let's spend some time in Scripture to see this principle of abundance in action. We're going to Genesis 26. Here we find Isaac, one of the patriarchs. He's arguably the least known patriarch. He's got a famous dad, Abraham who is the Father of our faith. Abraham is the one to whom Jehovah said, "I am going to cut covenant with you." Likely the only memory Isaac had of that God story was when the knife was coming at his throat as he lay on top of a stack of wood on a mountaintop. I would like to hear his perspective on that experience one day.

Not only was Isaac's father famous, so was his son, Jacob. Jacob would wrestle with an angel, who most scholars believe was the Lord. After the wrestling match, Jacob walked with a limp, and a nation was birthed. It was a pretty big story, but it doesn't end there. Isaac's grandson, Joseph, is one of the most famous people in all Scripture. As for Isaac himself, he was pretty ordinary. He gets less airtime than any of the other patriarchs— only one very short chapter. If anyone deserved to have orphan thinking, it was this guy. Famous dad, famous son, really famous grandson, and . . . Isaac, little bitty Isaac in one passage in Genesis. Fortunately, God's blessing doesn't just flow to the famous. God's blessing flows to all His children. The only thing that can stop it from manifesting in our lives is incorrect thinking about His nature.

Isaac faced a time of famine, just as his father did. He went to Abimelech, king of the Philistines and Gerar, and the Lord appeared to Isaac and said, "Do not go down to Egypt." That warning from God should sound very familiar. God's people seem to always be drawn to Egypt. The Father probably has a repeat button in heaven with the warning, "Do not go down to Egypt." Why is that? Because Egypt represents bondage. We would rather accept a form of spiritual slavery that is familiar to us than experience the unknown freedom available from God. We're like an elephant tied to a stick.

God also told Isaac: "Live in the land where I will tell you." He didn't give Isaac much detail on this one. That's probably because the Father is not a big fan of clarity. By the way, does this not remind you of Abraham's story? God tells him, "I know you don't know who I am, but I'm going to bless you and I will bless those who bless you. I am for you. I'm going to cut covenant with you. Everything that I have is yours. You're going to be called my friend. All I need you to do is leave the land where you're currently living and go to the land which I will show you." (See Genesis 12) Now with Isaac, we have "Abraham Part Two." God says to Isaac, "My name is Jehovah. I spared your life many years ago. I thought about you before you were created in your mother's womb. I need you to not live here anymore. I need you to leave everything and go to the land which I will show you." (See Genesis 26) Not a lot of clarity there either.

THE POSTURE OF THE HEART

If God gives me clarity, there's no space in my life for us (God and me) to work out a deep level of trust. When there's a lot of clarity, I get lazy and I won't build trust. Most people become fat and lazy in success. It seems easier, for a lot of people, to steward a lack rather than a lot. The true mark of being a mature follower of God is that He can give you a lot and it will not even faze you. Have you realized that it's possible to be a multibillionaire and be more humble than someone who lives in poverty? It is possible, because the posture of the heart is everything.

After God told Isaac to go to the land He would show him, He gave him these promises:

"Stay in this land for a while and I'll be with you and will bless you." God's nature is to bless. The conversation on blessing is not about the blessing, it is about the One doing the blessing. Here's what I'm trying to say—if you believe that God truly desires to bless you, don't be shocked when you start walking with Him and He does it. All He is asking for is a little bit of cooperation, to let Him be the way He's wired to be. This truth regarding abundance really triggers the orphan spirit and especially the religious spirit. That's because the enemy wants to convince you that it's more worthy to walk in lack. If you think about it, that just doesn't make sense. Why would you want an okay marriage when your spouse can truly be your best friend? What if the only way you can get to a great marriage is not through Dr. Phil or Dr. Boo-Hoo, or any other trendy route? What if, instead of getting ten people to pray for you, you pray for your spouse? Quite simply, what if you walk so closely with the Father, that He is blessing your marriage?

In whom do you trust? Here is what many of us do; we start screaming at our checkbooks. "I command you to do this, I command you to do that." Maybe the better thing to say is, "I never deserved to get to this King's Table life, ever. I never deserved it, but now that I'm here, I cannot say "thank you" enough. You are the most amazing person I've ever met in my life. Your blessings are chasing me left and right. Surely goodness and mercy shall follow me all the days of my life. I cannot believe how good You are. I cannot believe how good You are. You are so good. We trust You." It's all about Him.

What if God gave you blessings that you weren't even asking for? I can't tell you the last time I've prayed for anything. The Father told us, at our church, that giving would double the year I taught on firstfruits. We did not chase down a marketing person, or pour oil on the offering baskets. We simply believed God and taught our people the principles of firstfruits from the Word. Our leadership, the staff and elders, were the first to commit to honor Him in this area. It is amazing to watch what God told you would happen, actually happen. If I am walking with God, I actually believe that if I seek first His Kingdom and His righteousness, all these things will be added. Seek Him first and things get added. That's how it works. For Abraham, for Isaac, and for us.

God had more to say to Isaac: "For to you and your descendants I will give all these lands" (Genesis 26:3b). God's plan of blessing went way beyond just Abraham and Isaac. God's blessing on your life is not for you only. What if you are in such deep friendship with God that your great-great-great grandson, whom you will never meet until you are in heaven, is still living off the back draft of your blessing? God's nature is to bless. He tells Isaac, "I will give all these lands and will confirm the oath I swore to your father Abraham." I still live off the blessings from Mama Jane. Her faithfulness in building friendship with God has brought a blessing to four generations— her siblings and peers, her son, her grandchildren and great grandchildren. Even when she was in her last days, she continued to bless others. One of her caregivers said she was the sweetest person to the end. How does that happen? It happens when your heart is the soil for His Word to grow and then the fruit you give to others is sweet. You give because you know that it is His nature in you. You can give because you are no longer living in the land of lack.

It's not about setting up a bunch of targets in our lives, things we need to believe for. We just need to believe that God is good and that He is a good giver. Let's chase Him and let all these other things chase us. If you run towards money, it will run from you. A lot of times, if you run towards community, community will scatter from you. A lot of people don't walk in community because they are not intimately connected to the Father. I honestly believe in the Western Church we have so created God in our own image we've lost sight of His true character. We don't worship golden calves, we worship our own work, goals, and plans. We chase the prosperity message to get our entitlements. The prosperity message is always being blessed by God to bless others, and it finds its roots in Genesis 12:1-3. It is the message of abundance. You can love because He loved you. You can give because you know He is a giver. You can heal the sick, because you know He wants His people well. He is generous, so we can be too.

When you are intimately connected to the Father, blessing just flows in every area of your life. I can prove this biblically. I've seen people healed and I don't even pray for healing. I just say, "Father, show them Your goodness." His goodness has no bounds. Why would I cast faith to believe something that is the opposite of His goodness? Did you know one of the words used for prosperity in the Old Testament is *dashen* and it can mean, "to make fat." Praise God, He understands me. I really did laugh when I saw that definition. Dashen—to make fat. I love how God is wired. God also told Isaac, "I will make your descendants as numerous as the stars in the sky." Why did He say that? Because that's just the way He is. There is a pattern going on in God's Kingdom, and it goes something like this; "Adam and Eve, I will bless you, go and multiply. Abram, I am going to bless you. Isaac, I am going to bless you. Jesus, go to the earth and redeem the curse of the law. What I started in Abraham, I am going to make better with you. I am going to make a new covenant and all peoples of the earth will be blessed through you, as long as they will just let Me be Me. Let Me be your Father, let Me bless you."

LIVING FROM AN ABUNDANCE MINDSET

There is nothing more ridiculous than a good God wanting to bless His kids, and having them say, "No." They say, "Father, this is not what I was taught about You, so take me to that $0.99 menu because I have to be responsible." Perhaps you should take your spouse to an excellent restaurant and apologize for being so responsible. Perhaps what heaven calls unbelief, we just call being responsible. A lot of times, in the world's eyes, what we call wisdom, God calls unbelief. Recently I was in downtown Greenville and I was shopping for a Camelbak backpack. I found one that I thought was overpriced. When I looked it up on Amazon, it was thirty dollars cheaper online. I walked out thinking, "I need to be wise with my money." A few minutes later I heard this from the Father, "Go back in there and buy that Camelbak. Invest in the economy of Greenville and speak a blessing over the store." It took me a little while to discern that this was God. I wanted to make sure I was not being irresponsible. I went back to that store and did what the Father told me to do, and in the next four days, over four hundred dollars was handed to me from two people. I heard the Father say, "Your obedience and abundance mindset triggered this blessing." Perhaps we need to rethink His thoughts on blessing.

Did Jesus really need to make that much wine at the wedding? Did He really need to help Peter catch that many fish? When a little kid handed Him fish and bread, He fed somewhere between 15,000 and 35,000 people . . . and there was food left over. You can't get to the end of Him. There's no end to His supply. Where He guides you, He will provide for you. So, if He's guiding you to something, step out there. If you step out where He is not guiding, that's not abundance, that's idiocy. He blesses you as you follow, as you go to the land He will show you. It is not the other way around where we say, "Bless me as I make my own plans and go where I want to go, because you are good." Do not be manipulative. Trust is not manipulative. Love is not manipulative.

God promised Isaac that through his offspring, all nations on earth would be blessed. So much blessing—that's His nature. Isaac made the same bad decision his dad had previously made. He thought the men in this new land might kill him to take his wife, Rebekah, because she was so beautiful. So, he told the king and everyone else that she was his sister. Years before, Abraham did this very thing. He thought strangers in a new land would kill him and take his wife—so he told them she was his sister. I guess the apple never falls too far from the tree. Don't limit God by only giving Him subsections of your life. Just simply say, "God bless me, in everything." What if when your kid is struggling with school you respond by blessing the brains of your child to be able to think the way they were created to think? Why? Because that is how God is wired. You can live in the blessing. You can speak blessings too.

The difference between a spiritual son and an orphan is that a spiritual son clings to the Word of the Lord no matter what while an orphan will back off the Word under pressure. That Word of the Lord is both rhema and logos. You can believe Him. If He says go, then go. If He says stay and plant crops, then stay and plant crops. King Saul became yesterday's man when he did not obey the Word of the Lord. Samuel said to Saul, "You have rejected the word of the LORD, and the LORD has rejected you as king over Israel!" (1 Samuel 15:26). This is not a small matter. Elijah did much the same thing. On Mount Carmel he called down fire from heaven. In the very next scene, Jezebel was trying to kill him and he was scared to death. Isaac acted like an orphan, he failed to trust the Word of God and trust the blessing even in circumstances that seemed dangerous. He chose to be his own protector, his own wise counsel.

Sons and daughters stay at the table. You can reach a point with God where you remain at the Table because of the great revelation of His love and character, not because you have an epic encounter. You simply know God said it, and you stay put until He gives the next direction. Encounters are great. But I prefer revelation. With revelation, I change and I grow. Even Jesus grew in wisdom and revelation. Do you know that you can actually grow to a place in the Father, where encounters are not the most climactic point of your journey? His revelation trumps an encounter.

BE A MAMA JANE

When Isaac went away from the Word, what did God do? Did He kill him? No. "When Isaac had been there a long time, Abimelech king of the Philistines looked down from the window and saw Isaac caressing his wife Rebekah. (In the King James it says they were "sporting." I think it is the only time I have ever blushed reading the bible.) "So Abimelech summoned Isaac and said, 'She is really your wife! Why did you say, 'She is my sister'? Isaac answered him, 'Because I thought I might lose my life on account of her'" (Genesis 26:8-9). Spiritual orphans always have a reason for why they were not obedient. I would rather die at the King's Table in obedience to His Word than scheme my way through life. So Abimelech said, "What have we done? One of the men might well have slept with your wife and you would've brought guilt upon us." So, Abimelech gave orders to all the people, "Anyone who harms this man or his wife shall surely be put to death."

In the middle of our biggest mistakes, God's blessings still flow. How did the blessing flow here? He protected Rebekah and Isaac. God will do the same for us, even when we creep back into orphan land. The moment we realize what we're doing, we need to just stop and come back to the Table. We need to say, "I am sorry. I should have believed Your Word." We need to have community in our lives, so that whenever we're prone to drift and wander from our identity, we have someone who can say, "Whoa, whoa, whoa. You are talking like Lo-debar again. Why are you are talking like Lo-debar? Take those grave clothes back off please." It's so important to have those people in our lives who love us enough to speak truth. We tend to head back to Egypt and grab those grave clothes. Can you hear Father hitting the repeat button, "Do not go down to Egypt"? It is a high level of sonship to say, "I'm done with that forever. I'm done." You can always find excuses why you shouldn't step out when the Father calls you to step out. But you have to get past that. It comes down to this. What is the Father calling you to do? Once you hear from Him, anything other than obedience is unbelief, and He equates unbelief with witchcraft and murder. So, just step out and obey Him.

What if, because of your intimacy with the Father, you understood that He would protect you from things that you did not even know could come against you? Read Psalm 91 and believe it. It's about favor and blessing in the midst of warfare. My enemies are defeated by God Almighty before they can even get to me. What if, instead of you interceding, "Father, show me the 10 things I should fight," God says, "Just give me this battle and give me the next 11 battles, and I will fight those for you." He is faithful and His nature is to bless. He prepares a feast in the presence of our enemies. He fights for us.

"Isaac planted crops in that land and the same year reaped a hundredfold, because the LORD blessed him. The man became rich, and his wealth continued to grow until he became very wealthy. He had so many flocks and herds and servants that the Philistines envied him. So all the wells that his father's servants had dug in the time of his father Abraham, the Philistines stopped up, filling them with earth. Then Abimelech said to Isaac, 'Move away from us; you have become too powerful for us'" (Genesis 26:12-16). What if you stayed humble to the end, and the blessings of the Lord were so apparent on your life that the enemy's camp couldn't even stand looking at you? What if it were possible for you, as a wife and a mom raising children, to have so much favor on you because you sit at the Table, that it flows into your family? There's no "what if" to it. It is possible. You can be the Mama Jane, the matriarch that brings blessings to the future generations. No matter what you have lived through, you can be the blessing for your current generation and those to come.

Chapter 9

THE POWER OF LIFE
AT THE TABLE

FULLY DEPENDENT ON HIM

As a child, I was terrified of the enemy. When I was 5 years old, I saw into the spiritual realm one night, and what I saw scared me to death. I saw a green witch flying on a broomstick and I saw the nastiest looking gargoyle character I can describe. I sweated so much out of fear that I drenched my bed. I never told my parents because I did not want them to think I was crazy.

We need to be careful when we dismiss the things our children say as "fictitious." Kids see things that adults don't see. As a parent, I have had to go to war in prayer in my children's rooms a few times over things they were experiencing at night while they slept. All three of my children have told my wife and me a couple of times over the years that they sensed something bad in their rooms. We don't take this lightly because we know that the demonic realm is real.

What I saw in my room as a 5-year old was as real as anything I've ever seen.

I have been privileged to lead teams to Haiti six times with Gary Hyppolite and Bethel Mission Outreach who are global partners with Bridgeway Church. These have been wonderful opportunities for me to learn from Gary and help him with whatever he needs to fulfill what God has called him to do. I recall one trip in particular. On this trip, Gary asked if we would like to go on a treasure hunt in the downtown area. I was excited because I absolutely love going on treasure hunts to see what Holy Spirit will do. The thing I love about treasure hunts is that you absolutely have to hear God and act on what He says without "processing" it for weeks and months beforehand. I think that much of the over-planning we do is nothing more than unbelief and the inability to hear the Father's voice and trust Him. The word "processing" has become a hipster word in many circles, and I'm convinced that what we call "processing" God calls "unbelief" most of the time. God told Abram to pick up his family and move. He said "yes," and moved. No processing required. I always want to be responsible with what the Father is telling me or the team which I am leading, because if we are not careful, we will take way too long to do what He is asking us to do.

We got on the bus and headed to downtown Croix-des-Bouquets. When we got to the center of town, our team walked over to a basketball court. I immediately heard Holy Spirit tell me to pray for a young man who was a vendor selling water and rice. On his head was an enormous bag that looked incredibly heavy. I told our interpreter Christopher to ask the young man if he had pain in his neck, back and knees. The young man said he did. Right there in the square I prayed for him, and God healed him. This young man told our interpreter that all the pain had left his body. The Holy Spirit told me to pray, I prayed, and the supernatural became more real than the natural in that moment. We hugged this young man, and then Gary said that he wanted us to walk a little bit down the road to the town square where there were more people.

So, after praying for the water and ice vendor, and seeing God heal him, we headed towards Town Square. When we turned the corner and stepped into the Square, I saw "him"—a witch doctor standing on the corner. Our interpreter immediately said, "Don't look at him. Just keep walking." I could tell that some on our team were a little scared. This man had a toy dragon in his hands and different odd ornament necklaces on his neck. The presence of evil emanating from him was very easy to detect. Things were getting real in a hurry.

Voodoo is rampant in Haiti. Where I live in Greenville, there's a place called Voodoo BBQ. I would never choose a name like that because I have come to understand just how real and demonic voodoo is. Most Americans don't understand this spiritual reality. As a matter of fact, many Christians think it's silly to even talk about such things. I've heard people say, "You charismatics love the drama of stuff like that." It's not drama. Ask Gary. He knows voodoo is nothing to play around with. Gary would not be allowed to preach in many churches in America because the congregations would either not believe his stories or would simply not want to entertain the idea of such things.

As our team walked around the witch doctor, he began to hiss at us. He did this three times. Christopher our interpreter said, "Let's walk quickly to the square. Don't look at him." At this point, I was in the back of the line, with the entire team of 15 people in front of me. I stopped, turned around and stared at this guy. It made me so angry that the enemy was influencing a man to taunt the team I was leading. As I stared at him, all I could think of was, "the one who is in you [me] is greater than the one who is in the world." (See 1 John 4:4) Christopher asked me, "Do you think the Lord has something for him?" I said, "Yep, let's go." You see, there comes a time when we must simply either believe in the power of life at the Table or not. Not everything is gray. Christianity has to be more than clever whiteboard sessions centered on doctrine and leadership. It has to take action—even in the face of fear. We have to realize that we are working in God's power, not our own; that we are fully dependent on Him.

Christopher and I walked up to the steps where this man was standing. Only one time in my life have I felt a stronger sense of evil. The Lord told me clearly as I was walking up to this man that this was not a situation to play around with. The Lord said, "Chad, he is high-ranking in the demonic." When we walked up to him, he looked right at Christopher, the Haitian interpreter, and said something I could not understand. Christopher looked at me and said, "I'm dizzy. What's going on?" In that moment, I completely snapped with righteous indignation. I looked right at Christopher and said, "I command this dizziness to stop. Father, I ask that You manifest Your presence right now." Instantly, Chris was no longer dizzy. I could tell that something rose up in him too.

I must have said the name of Jesus 40 times over the next 15 minutes. Then I began to pray in the Spirit, which really agitated the witch doctor. I never had any hatred toward the man, but I was furious with the enemy who was influencing him. I couldn't care less how high he ranked in the enemy's camp. In that moment, I did not pray for God to increase my courage or give me revelation of who I am. Sometimes you don't need to pray—you need to simply act. I knew that greater is He who is in me than he who is in the world. I also knew that the same power that is in me raised my King from the grave. (See Romans 8:11) I was locked in at the Table and I realized that the Lion of Judah was alive and well, and all I had to do was release the power that was already in me. When I did this by declaring the Gospel to this man, his demeanor changed. There was no more hissing going on. He would not look me in the eye, and his agitation increased. Paul said that the Gospel is not a matter of talk but of power. The power of God made Christopher's dizziness go away and made the demeanor of this man soften and bow quickly.

I wish I could say that he decided to leave his life of witchcraft and accept Jesus as his savior. He did not do that on that day. I can say that the Gospel was shared with him and it was obvious that he realized he had no power over the unseen Jesus that day. As we talked through this experience as a team, I could tell that quite a few team members realized that the idea of Jesus in us is more real than theory. It's one thing to preach that Jesus is in you. It's quite another thing to believe in that reality and step in the face of a witch doctor steeped in voodoo to prove it. This happened early in the trip, and I noticed that quite a few team members wanted to fight through their own fears and step into who the Father desired them to be throughout the rest of the trip.

Faith is not the absence of fear and doubt. It is stepping right through fear and doubt and moving past what comes against us in our own thoughts. At the time Christopher was getting dizzy in the witch doctor's presence, I had massive thoughts of fear come at me—the kind I have not dealt with in years. At one point, I could feel that dreaded sense of fear in the natural realm. Faith is not waiting till these things are gone. It's simply moving right through our own doubts and fear to step into the place of authority and identity that is ours at the King's Table. It's understanding that our own power will fail, but His power will not. We can only operate in this level of power when we are fully dependent on Him. We all have fears, we all have misconceptions, things that we believe that do not align to truth, but we believe them nonetheless. We have blind spots. What we think about ourselves may not align with the truth, both in areas that are strengths and weaknesses for us. We need our Father who art in heaven, we need our big brother, Jesus, we need our helper, Holy Spirit, and we need family and community.

I believe we make a lot of excuses from ignorance and not out of rebellion. We aren't free because we either don't know the truth or we choose to not believe it. Changing our thinking and moving from being crippled by fear, anxiety and misconceptions requires that we open ourselves up to others and to community. When I say "open up," I am not saying to become a punching bag for every slander and punch someone wants to throw at you. I am saying that we should be open and vulnerable to others, and when we are, it can lead to even greater understanding of how Father created us and His plan for us. When He searches our hearts, He isn't just searching for the flaws, He is searching for the dreams He has set in us since before we were a glimmer in our earthly dad's eyes.

Some of the excuses we make come from the hurts we experienced from people we should have been able to trust. We make excuses for our own behaviors based on our family trees saying things like, "My daddy was angry, my granddad was angry, and I am angry." We are just angry people at times because of a lack of revelation. I think what could be very helpful is to understand what happened at the cross, and how we are made new when the Spirit of Christ dwells in us. When you accepted Christ and invited Him to reside in you, when you died to your own flesh and then walked on the waters of baptism, when His victory became your own victory, you left the old behind. We need to stop looking at our old family tree as an excuse and start looking to our new family tree and live from there. Your heavenly Father props His feet on the moon. Your big brother Jesus conquered death bringing you abundant life and the power to live and to do your Father's works. I know which family tree I want to live from.

I have decided to pull from the legacy of love that is available to me as a believer and leave behind the old. How do we do that? Forgiveness. When Jesus hung on the cross, beaten beyond recognition, He said, "Forgive them, for they know not what they do" (Luke 23:34 ESV). Forgiveness is not an excuse. It releases us from the sins of another, and the shame of another, and from our own poor choices. Forgiveness is the path to the freedom. It is the way to open yourself to begin to think like your Father, to see from His perspective and not from your wounds. It is a true transformation that goes beyond just moving out of Lo-debar. It is the art of remaining at the Table; the art of building deep friendship with Elohim. It is the ongoing dance; the poem that He continues to write that is the story of your life that brings light into the darkness. It is life lived vulnerably in community without excuses. It is owning your mistakes and saying, "I am sorry," and then working toward not repeating that behavior again. This might sound like striving, but it is really all about not sitting back and waiting for something you have already been given.

The apostle Paul wrote that we are to work out our salvation with fear and trembling. (See Philippians 2:12) He is talking about Holy Fear, a fear of God who is our Father, whose ways are higher than our own understanding; a fear of God who is the Ancient of Days and knows before He speaks just how He intends the story to unfold. My reverence for Him is my trust in His goodness that is built over time. If you let Him, He will take you again and again into deeper levels of trust, not because of fear, but because as you grow in wisdom and revelation, you are trusted with even greater things. He shares His secrets with His friends. You grow to trust Him and He sees in you a trustworthy son. Trust is built, not given.

LIVING WITH TRUTH TELLERS

We all need a few trusted people in our life who will tell us the truth. I like to refer to the truth tellers in my life as "chocolate-covered razor blades." They get the job done in the sweetest way. I have three. These are people that when I ask them a question or they see me taking on an offense, or acting in a way that is unloving, they call me out. I may not be from a family of runners, but I am in a family of truth tellers. Hear me say this, truth telling is calling out who you are in the Family of God, how He made you—calling out His character in you, His truth. These truth tellers have a critical eye, not a critical spirit. We need people in our life who love us and tell us the truth, based on the Word of God and not their own opinions. They are put in our life to help us develop. King Saul had an assignment, but because of his pride, his ambition, his appetites, and his desire for the approval of man, he failed to see that he was getting off course. God puts us in relationship with others so we don't boast of anything other than how much we know Him. It is a fact. I want to please my heavenly Father, and sometimes He works through others to help me develop the character needed to fulfill my assignment.

Truth tellers are motivated by love. They are not trying to damage you or break you. They want to help you grow and see you succeed. Truth tellers are patient and know that you are always a work in progress. They are kind and they leave you with hope. They are not envious, trying to break you in order to elevate themselves. They don't boast of how much they "helped" you, or gossip about you or others. They take no pride in their words. Truth tellers love well and are not afraid to help you see through God's eyes and heaven's perspective. They trust God to only reveal what you need to know in the moment. Our big brother, Jesus modeled this. He spent time with Father, then moved out to love others in power. He left people with hope because He was moved by compassion. He didn't see the woman at the well as a project to fix, like a leaky toilet that had soiled the floor. He saw her as a daughter who had lost her way, believing untruths. When she met Jesus, He told her the truth without destroying her in the process. He reminded her of her identity and set her free. We need wise people around us who know what is required of us, who act justly, love mercy and walk humbly with God everyday (Micah 6:8), who help us see our excuses as feeble veils keeping us from the truth. Jesus removed the veil so that we can have direct access to Him. Access to Jesus is access to the truth.

So how do we know the truth? How do we know if what these chocolate-covered razor blades are saying is true? We have two ways to weigh and measure, to judge truth. One is the Word of God, and the other is the life of Jesus. We have been given the great gift of the Holy Spirit. It was through Him that the Word of God was put into written form. Jesus was the Word made flesh, before the earth was even formed. He only did what He saw the Father do, He only spoke what He heard the Father say. He told us to judge the fruit. We can know that the truth tellers in our life are trustworthy by their fruit. Jesus knew the Torah very well; he was a student of the Word, setting an example for us to also be students of the Word. Holy Spirit will always align you to the Word. He is our present day comforter and the power in our life. If the words in your head and heart do not align with the Word and the Spirit, they aren't from God. Set your mind on the truth and you will find a freedom that is too good to be true. The Gospel message of love is for you today. It heals your past and gives hope to your future and the future generations.

THE BENEFITS OF SONSHIP

We can learn a lot from past generations. People like my grandparents, who lived through a world war, learned to be content in their "today." They learned to take on the responsibilities they were given with determination and grit. They fought for freedom, living without entitlement. They lived in a place few of us in the West have had to live. Not knowing what tomorrow would bring, they loved well in the moment and held loosely to their possessions, living to love their neighbors because they understood their current conditions were not their forever story. The joy of each new morning was their "happily ever after." Sounds like Psalms and Proverbs doesn't it, like the early church in Acts, like the Kingdom of God. It sounds like sonship.

Micah 6:8 says, "He has told you, O man, what is good; and what does the LORD require of you but to do justice, and to love kindness, and to walk humbly with your God?" This kind of living comes at a price. We don't just turn around one day flowing with loving kindness, humility and a heart's desire for Kingdom justice. More often than not, God has to speak to us just to get our attention about these things. You may be surprised by how He chooses to speak to you. If God could speak through a donkey, maybe just maybe He can speak through your spouse or your children. When He speaks, we need to be able to listen with humility, turn over what is said and then make adjustments. That means no more excuses when it comes to issues of pride. Pride can take us to a place where we compare ourselves to others and we keep chasing perfection in order to be the best. Pride can disguise our need for other people and keep us self-reliant. Pride can keep you from being able to receive, skewing your perspective of the Father. Pride can tell us we do not need this "religious stuff," that we are good just as we are. I'm among the first to say that we do not need religious stuff. We need the One whose name is on the front door. Too often it seems we have lost Jesus Christ in a religion that carries His name. I see people who have come out of Lo-debar and still remember the stench with a greater understanding of Christ than those who have followed religion and grown apathetic and cold. I think that Holy Spirit is busy reintroducing Christians to Christ once again because we need a reintroduction.

One way to limit God is to be our own enemy, a stubborn mule who chooses excuses over change, believing that change is not possible. I want to live my life in obedience. God is my goal. I don't want to limit Him by my thoughts, or misconceptions, or pride. I want to build on His truths. I want to stop making excuses. We have a Papa who calls Himself "Love." Each one of us has been bought with a love gift of blood so that we can be free. We have Holy Spirit in inside of us, with us at all times. It is time to come to the family table, to receive the benefits of being in the family. What is available to us at the Table is for our benefit, the benefit of our family, our marriage, and our friendships. It is for the benefit of our city, our nation and all the nations of the world. We get to live with the benefits of sonship.

GOING DEEPER WITH GOD

As a pastor, I have noticed that we have a tendency to place blame on someone else when things don't go well in life instead of taking responsibility for our own decisions and behaviors. In counseling sessions I will hear things like, "If my mother would have raised me different then I would not be like this. If my spouse was more sold out to God then things would be different. If I had a stronger community then these things would not be happening in my life." The moment we decide that we are responsible for our own development is the moment that our life changes. In my twenty years of pastoral ministry, I have not seen significant and lasting personal growth happen unless the person is willing to take responsibility for his or her own life. One of my favorite passages in the Bible is when Jesus asks the man who has been sick for 38 years, "Do you want to get well?" (John 5:6). At 29 years of age I was overcome with anxiety in a fetal position on the floor. A year later I saw blind eyes open. What I came to understand was that the blame game is really a denial of our identity in Christ. An angel did not manifest to get me out of a fetal position and off the kitchen floor. I was able to get off the floor because I began taking hundreds of truths of who I was in Christ and living from what the Father said was true about me. I picked up my mat and walked. If you can go another week without seeing someone healed through your hands, you will. If you can go another week without growing in the prophetic, you will. If you continue to make excuses of why you do not currently have deep friendship with God, then a year from now you will find yourself in the same exact position with the Father. May you rise up in courage and make the decision to never make another excuse for why you don't have what you have with the Father. His love and kindness has an amazing way of transforming our passion and courage. (See Romans 2:4) May this be the season where you declare war on any excuse you have for why you are lacking in friendship with God.

Chapter 10

THE CHARACTER
OF JESUS

I **TRAVELED FOR FIFTEEN YEARS** to serve God and make a living for our family. When you travel somewhere and speak to fifty or even five thousand people, you are a hero. They don't get offended with you because you're only with them for a few days. You are a rock star, like Bono. It's not the same when you come back home. It's really not the same when you pastor a church. That rock star effect isn't there when you are preaching and teaching and doing life with people who are very familiar with you.

When I took the job as the Lead Pastor of Bridgeway Church, no one, not even God, gave me a heads-up. I could have used one because He taught me, in the first three years of pastoring, that many Christians in the church walk in a high level of offense on a daily basis. This is a very uncomfortable truth that we have to deal with in the church. I'm not just talking about your spouse or all the lost souls out there. I'm talking to all of us. If you wonder where you are on the sliding scale between Lo-debar and the King's Table, there is one ginormous question that can lead you to your answer. How easily are you offended? I'm talking about being offended in every area of your life—home, work, church, family, travel, community—all of it. How strong is the spirit of offense in your life?

Now, think about this next question. How easily offended was Jesus? They beat Him beyond recognition. Most scholars believe you could barely tell He was human because He was beaten so badly. That would seem like a pretty good cause for offense. Yet, with His last breath, with teeth probably broken or missing, and with a bloody mouth, He prayed, "Forgive them, they don't know what they're doing. Abba, forgive them." (See Luke 23:34) That is how Jesus Christ handled offense. As a Christian—a Christ-follower—that is the lead we should follow. Being a Christian is more than just going to heaven when we die. Jesus came to the earth to reconnect us to Eden, to reconnect us to His Father, to provide us a seat at the King's Table. He is the bridge to Father. If I'm with Him at the King's Table, am I really going to be walking around every day offended? If your answer is anywhere in the realm of "yes," then you are likely headed back toward Lo-debar, if not still living there.

IT TAKES COMMUNITY

The things that I am sharing with you are not just theories. I have lived through this. The story of offense is my story. The friends I did life with twenty years ago would probably not believe it if they heard me talking about getting over it, about not living in offense. Back then, you could look at me wrong and I got offended. If you said something negative, it would take me two weeks to get over it. What I am sharing with you is very real to me. Go with me to the desert for a moment if you will. In Matthew 4, we find Jesus hungry and weak, and the enemy is there to tempt Him. Satan came at Jesus in three ways: he came after His ambition, His appetite, and His need for approval. I always thought that my big struggle was appetite. Going to Moe's for me is a big deal. Seriously, I get excited about cheese dip. If I looked at the three temptations Jesus faced—ambition, appetite, approval—I would have said, "well, my weakness is appetite, no doubt." Struggling with ambition did not register with me, even when I was processing this with the Father. I could have put my hand on a lie detector test and declared that, "The approval thing in me is dead." I had a serious blind spot, which is why we need community. You are not as good-looking as you think you are, and you are not as smart as you think you are. I don't care how close to the Father you think you are, sometimes you need the Holy Ghost, Jesus, the Father, His angelic revelation, *and* your friends to call a timeout in your life. This is true for everyone, especially me.

I wouldn't be surprised if Father has said to the Holy Spirit, "Let Me talk to Chad," and then Father went back to the Holy Spirit and said, "Let's get Jesus involved with this one, and even a little angelic ministry. And you know what else? I am going to breathe on four or five of his friends and they are going to talk to him too, about this approval thing." The whole time this conversation was going on, I was just there talking about sonship, and the healing that comes from recognizing your identity as a son, and how much Father loves you. I was totally unaware of my own glaring blind spot. When it comes to breakthrough, there is nothing more embarrassing and nothing more amazing than for God to show you something about yourself that you literally don't see. It seems to me that amazing should beat embarrassing every time. I believe that embarrassment is why people avoid community. They may say, "God is just calling me to be alone in this season." No, He is not. God is not alone; He is plural. God is community. He said, "Let *us* make man in *our* image." The Lord may want you by yourself for a couple of days, but let's not make that thirty-two years. Sooner or later, you have to ask the question, "Where am I?" and be willing to hear the answer. "Where am I? Am I worshiping the Father in a corporate setting but wearing grave clothes the whole time? Am I singing for something I want, but there is no evidence of it in my life?" Sometimes the things you preach the hardest and you talk about the most are the very things you're reaching for because you don't currently have them. For example, I preached this passage about 18 months prior to my blind spot being revealed and I had no idea it was about me.

THE THIN PLACE

> *"Just as Jesus was coming up out of the water, he saw heaven being torn open and the Spirit descending on him like a dove."*
>
> *Mark 1:10*

What if tomorrow morning, you're going about your normal day, and heaven opens up, you hear an audible voice, and the Spirit descends upon you? That is a dramatic God encounter. I had a tremendously abnormal encounter with God in 2014. I didn't come up out of water to see heaven opening. As a matter of fact, I was just in my den. It was 2:30 in the morning, my wife was asleep on the couch and I was typing. We even had a fire going because it was winter. It was a great Nicholas Sparks type moment. I'm not being casual about this because I do not hear the audible voice of God all the time. Angels don't manifest in my room on a rhythmic pattern. If you hang around me, you'll find I'm actually quite boring. So, what I'm about to describe to you isn't something that happens every Thursday afternoon. It has only happened to me one other time in my life, and that was on June 4, 1994. It's so uncommon that I remember the specific dates.

The encounter started when I heard an audible voice while I was in my den, and I knew who it was. The first thing He said was, "Put your computer down." Then He told me what He was about to do in my life. I didn't cry. I didn't shake. I didn't fall down. I didn't yell. I simply said, "Why?" I'm not going into all that He shared with me about my assignment. It simply is not wise to talk about everything He shares with you. I probably will at the end of my life, if I stay clean and pure and watch everything He shared that morning come to pass. But in that moment, I just said, "Why?" And He said... nothing. However, a tangible love came over me. Have you ever started crying because you just know you're accepted by God? Sometimes it happens in worship. You know everything's going to be okay. In the moment you're not suicidal, but you wish you could just get sucked up into a vortex and go to heaven. By the way, if we don't get homesick for heaven from time to time we are probably not walking with Him—we are mostly just believing in Him. We have a place at the Table but you're living in Lo-debar. For two and a half weeks, I was in what some call "the thin place." It doesn't happen all the time with me. But, for those two and a half weeks, I could not stop thinking about Him and He didn't stop talking to me. He showed me my future, He showed me my assignment, He showed me what to do. And . . . He tested me. I was having an awesome dramatic God encounter. I had no idea what was about to happen.

KNUCKLEBALLS

"And a voice came from heaven:
"You are my Son, whom I love; with you I am well pleased."
Mark 1:11

It was a year and a half after that dramatic encounter in my den before I realized that what I am about to share with you did not come from the enemy, it came from our loving Father. He intentionally did something in my life that I thought was the work of the enemy. He wanted to expose a lot of Lo-debar in me. I didn't see it coming, and I was the pastor of a church. It is humbling to be following God hard and then get thrown a knuckleball when you're used to hitting softballs. If I lob you a soft ball, you can probably hit it; but if I throw you a Tim Wakefield knuckleball, you'll probably jump out of the way and get Strike One. The ball will move all over the place. When that happens spiritually, it can make you wonder what is going on. You may just want to jump out of the way. God had to throw a knuckleball at me to get me to see that I was using the language of the King's Table but there was something hidden in my own heart, and that "thing" was 100% orphan thinking. It wasn't a small thing either. It was a big thing.

God threw His best Tim Wakefield knuckleball at me and then He said, "Chad, I love you enough to tell you I cannot do *through* you, what I have not first done in you. Quit praying for the devil to get off your back. I'm going to prune you so hard because I have to get Lo-debar out of you and show you that you *talk* about the King's Table more than you *live* at it." God was about to tell me that I was walking in offense and that it was time to prune it off. I knew I used to walk in it, but I thought it was killed in me. Dead and gone. It wasn't. For two and half weeks after my big encounter in the den, I was in a thin place and it was amazing. I could have lived there for the rest of my life. I was clear about my assignment. I had zero doubts. Then one by one the Father started leading people out of my life that I was very close to and did life with. Seven guys that I did life with on a weekly basis left the Church I pastor. We very rarely saw each other much after that. When I watched them walk away, something I didn't even know existed bubbled up from my heart. Then I did what most of us do, especially guys. I kept my John Wayne face on and pushed that thing right back down where it came from. Trouble is, that doesn't work long-term. When something is bubbling in your heart, it's not a matter of whether it's bubbling, it's a matter of whether you will deal with what's being exposed. You see, spiritual orphans think that God exposes things to punish us and condemn us. But that's not true. It is pure grace and pure love that motivates Him to expose these things in us. When my friends left our church, I started picking up on vibes from the Father that said, "You need to prepare for some bumpy waters, and it doesn't have anything to do with anyone else in your life. The bumpy waters concern your heart. This isn't about your wife, and it isn't about your kids. This isn't about your assignment or your friends. Chad, I love you enough to tell you that you have such a big blind spot in you that, if I don't help you and if I don't heal you of this, you will never be able to fulfill your assignment."

What does offense look like? I don't think anyone would ever admit to every bit of this language, but here are some thoughts we all have, even though we might not say them out loud:

- You hurt my feelings.

- I feel betrayed.

- I'm going to harbor unforgiveness for a long time.

- I can't stand even the thought of you.

- I will judge you, condemn you, avoid you, and even slander you.

- How dare you hurt me, you will never hurt me again.

- I am disappointed in you. You did not meet my expectations.

While some of those sound ridiculous to say out loud, there are probably a few that hit really close to home. When my friends left our church, my offended heart didn't match the way I was speaking with my mouth. My offense manifested with me being silent, internalizing the pain, and thinking it was all about me. I felt abandoned. How could they leave me? I will never forget the day the Father said, "Chad, you've never been the point of your own narrative." Isn't it interesting how God can say difficult things to us and yet we sense His tenderness as He relays what's on His mind?

So, there I was—using Table language but living like a spiritual orphan off and on. I did not want to stay there, so I started making my way back to the King's Table. I started growing in friendship with the Father. Then He said, "Chad, there is one more deathblow I need to give to you. Luke

9:23 is going to be both your best friend and your worst friend for a while, because you think it has started, but it hasn't started yet." At times like these you can be tempted to lean back into Lo-debar because you're actually seeking the approval of those closest to you more than you are seeking obedience to God's approval. When God said that to me … well, you can't exactly say, "Get behind me Satan" when you hear things like that from God. I knew it was Him—His sheep hear His voice.

STARVING UNTO DEATH

When you squeeze a lemon, lemon juice comes out. When Father squeezes a Christian, often offense comes out. I want the Father to squeeze me and I want Jesus to come out. There was only one way He could get me to the place where He could squeeze me and Jesus would come out more. He didn't accomplish this by telling me how great I was. He did it by taking me into a desert and starving me of the things I thought I needed. He started to open up my eyes by asking, "Why do you act a different way around certain people? Why do you strive for the approval of so many people?" I said, "Just kill me, just kill me." The deathblow was coming. Have you ever gone through a season where the Father is quiet on purpose, because He is starving something in you?

Then I was given another strong prophetic word from a prophet who lives out of state. I didn't know whether I wanted to fight him or run from him. He said, "God's been chipping away at you, but this last thing is the deathblow. If you will open yourself up, He wants to kill this thing before anything happens in your life." When He said that, I almost didn't want to receive it. But I needed to. The truth is, if you are in a deep level of Lo-debar, sometimes the best thing Father can do is to not caress you out of it. Sometimes the best thing Father can do is to starve you of whatever's in you that is not supposed to be there. It isn't about making you feel terrible about yourself. The whole purpose of what you are going through is to be groomed into the image of Jesus Christ. It is not your platform. It is not your gift. It is not your family. It is not your destiny. It is this simple question, "Are you growing in the image of Jesus, the most selfless human to ever live?" Until I get to a place of selflessness, I can believe in Him, but I'm not one with Him. Let's get real, we're all selfish. We all get offended. I am growing. I am allowing Him to show me my blind spots, even when it hurts. I want my heart to be like His. I want to love others like He does. The only one who can change is me. It all started with that simple prayer— "Search my heart." For me, the best thing that could have happened to me was to have the people that I was very close to leave and not be in my life anymore on a regular basis. What I thought was the enemy stirring up conflict in my life was a loving Father's pleasure to groom me for something He wanted to do through me. I am a firm believer that God will remove any crutch in our lives that takes the place of only what He wants to fulfill. The need for approval from others was something that was driving my life and I did not even know it.

If we run towards our destinies without having the character of Jesus, it can end up disastrous. If God puts His hand on Bridgeway and it helps many people, but I have an obsession with approval, I'll be done within one to two years. Approval, appetite and ambition are never satisfied. You have to continually feed them to feel content. Even though my blind spot had to do with approval, the same principles apply for any stumbling block. If you are man enough or woman enough, if you are tired of feeding your own needs, then do something. Just ask the Father what's inside of you that needs to be exposed and let Him deal with it. Let Him be the gardener; don't tell Him how to prune you. I have never seen a crepe myrtle say, "Hey take it easy, Hoss." The crepe myrtle just needs to say, "Oh boy," and know that if the Father wants to prune it so low that it looks like a stump, then He's only doing it because He deems it worthy of explosive growth. The same is true when the Father prunes us. Growth only comes through death. Hear me out: your spouse is not your problem. Your boss is not your problem. Your friends are not the problem. Many times, the enemy is not your problem. You know who the problem is? The guy or gal in the mirror. When the Father starts pruning, here is what orphans say: "Well, I knew it. You hate me, that's why You're pruning me. You hate me. You're only pointing out bad things to me." I was in that place. But God, through tears, was saying to me, "Chad, if you will just let Me do this, you have no idea of the fruit you'll bear. If you will just let me do this you will get to enjoy the fruit. You must allow me to take the blade to the root if you want to enjoy the fruit." This is how it works in the Kingdom. You have fruit that is growing until the day He comes to prune you. Pruning does not just happen once in your lifetime, or in only one area of your life. As you permit Him to prune you, to remove your own selfishness. Then, over seasons of pruning and growth, you will grow into a mighty oak tree. Remember the mighty oaks of righteousness planted by streams of living water. When you've grown into a mighty oak, people can come and take shade under your obedience to Him.

Everyone wants the identity and the promise that He is going to use us to do great things, yet few want to submit to the Father's pruning process. Very few really want God to squeeze them to see what comes out. It's the spiritual sons and spiritual daughters who just say, "You can have all of me. You can have all of me." They are the ones who bear fruit.

TRUSTING HIM

Things change when you give up offense. One of those spiritual sons who left called me. He had no idea I was writing about offense. We met at a restaurant, sat down, and he said, "I owe you." I told him that he owed me nothing. As a matter of fact, I owed him a "thank you." I told him that I owed all of them who left, a thank you. Later, as I got to thinking of those whose approval I had been seeking, I was reminded of everything God has been doing within me. I now realize that at the time of the exodus from Bridgeway, I just didn't know or understand what

God was doing. When you can't understand what He's doing, it's okay, just be patient. Trust Him beyond your own understanding.

If I plant potatoes and go out the next day and start screaming at them to grow, God is going to have to tell me that my method won't work. There's a thing called seedtime harvest. Wouldn't it be great if God just said, "Okay, I'm going to get all the Lo-debar out of you just by blowing on you, and just like that it will be done?" That's not how He does things. Realistically, it may take you two years to get rid of all your orphanhood thinking. You can't get there today, but you can start today by taking responsibility for yourself. Begin by saying, "God, I'm done with this. And while you're at it— while you're killing the approval thing, you might as well just kill the appetite thing, and kill the ambition thing too. Just kill it all. Kill it all." When you can do this, you can get to the end yourself and you can start to sound like Paul. You learn to be content in all things. You're no longer focused on the fruit. Someone can give you a compliment and you don't even feel it; you don't even hear it because you no longer need it. I am living proof of this. When I was a high-level orphan, I'd get offended if you just looked at me wrong. Now, sometimes I get compliments and I hardly even hear them. When we allow God to prune, transformation follows.

Only God can transform us. We can't transform ourselves. We can open ourselves and ask Him to search us and kill everything He doesn't want within us. Yet, we can't transform ourselves. The only thing that can help us is death at the cross, picking up our own cross, and following Him. When we do that, our stuff just starts falling off us. Paul was struck blind, went into the Arabian desert for three years and Jesus just pecked away at him. God said, "Paul, I am going to show you how much you must suffer for me." Paul was in a jail cell, about to be killed, but he wasn't drowning in offense. Instead, he was reflecting on just how good the Lord is. There's proof—you can get to the end of yourself. It is possible. It's a great day when you come to the end of yourself and you know that offense is being killed in you. When you're around people who used to offend you—perhaps it's even your ex-spouse—and you've got nothing but love and blessing for them, you'll know offense is being killed. The death of offense is a monumental thing.

FROM CONFLICT TO CHARACTER

I used to think that all conflict came from the enemy. Now, I think a lot of conflict is caused by the Father and we just think it's the enemy. Only in conflict do you truly find out who you really are. Conflict will also reveal the character of those around you. Without tension you do not have friends, you have acquaintances. Without conflict, you do not have a true family. Conflict transforms us. Conflict forces you to see what is in you that can be transformed into the image of Christ, who was the perfect representation of Father. As you are transformed, you find that you hold on to less. You can choose to be your own master, or owner, holding onto every offense and holding onto unforgiveness, or you can choose to let Him be the Master. When He is the Master, I can let Him groom me to forgive. I can let Him groom me to release offense. I release the need to be right. When that happens, I can have nothing but love for whoever I was in conflict with. The highest level of sonship is, "*Abba, forgive them for they do not know what they are doing.*"

People say to me often that they want community, but the truth is that we cannot have community if we are not willing to have conflict. The flip side is you really cannot grow without community. It is not just you and Jesus alone. It is you and Jesus and the rest of the family. If the goal is selflessness, the path to that selflessness runs through conflict, not peace. When I go through conflict, it makes me lean into the Father more. Perhaps what you're going through with your boss right now isn't from the enemy. What if the Father is grooming you through someone who doesn't even know Him? What would His purpose be in doing this? To groom you into the image of Jesus. He's not trying to groom you into the image of an author. He's not trying to groom you into the image of a leader. He's actually trying to groom you into the image of a follower of His Son. Everyone wants to lead but few want to follow. Let's say your life falls apart, but your character is growing in Jesus Christ. It seems like nothing is being blessed around you. However, He's telling you, "You're one of My closest friends." Do you care more about the abundance you feel is missing or the friendship you have with Him?

Paul's answer to that question is obvious from his life and writings. Paul went to Malta, healed everyone on the island, and shortly thereafter, when he knew it was the end of his life, he wrote in Philippians: "I just want to know You. I just want to know You, and the power of Your resurrection. I just want to know You." (See Philippians 3) He was saying all that as he was about to die.

If we're not careful, we will use the language of the King's Table and seem prosperous while we're actually living in Lo-debar. Back in the 1960s, cocaine was the addiction of choice. Now, in the 21st century, the addiction of choice is the "like" button on social media. We're addicted. We live our lives through the like button. What if God did something great through you and you said, "You know what, instead of telling the world how great I am right now, I'm just going to take a break?" This is not meant as condemnation. I'm just sharing my story, my journey. I've gone from lying in a fetal position on the kitchen floor to accepting this truth about life as a spiritual son at the King's Table. I wish I could tell you that the journey from Lo-debar to the King's Table is quick and easy, but I can't. Maybe the goal is to just keep coming to the Table. Don't stop coming to the Table. When you drop the ball and realize you've walked in a low level of offense for two years, don't beat yourself up. Instead, just say to the Father, "Why do I still have Lo-debar in me?" He wants you to keep coming to the Table. If you stay in Lo-debar, then you're defined by your depression, by your offense, by your anger. You are defined by words that are contrary to His Word, and to the culture of the

Kingdom and the family Table. You do not have to stay in Lo-debar. Just get up, like the lame man after 38 years, and say, "I can't do this anymore." When depression rears its head at you, when excuse rears its head, just say, "Enough! I declare war!" Then, put yourself in community and be big enough to ask those around you to speak into your life. Refuse to hide. Just keep coming to the Table. The invitation of this entire book is to let go of Lo-debar and come to the King's Table, leaving offense behind in the dust. No matter how difficult it seems, never stop coming to the Table. When the ideology of remaining at the Table becomes the norm for your life, you will see fruit and you will see your gifts grow.

Chapter 11

AWAKENING

Then he said to them all: 'Whoever wants to be my disciple must deny themselves and take up their cross daily and follow me.'

Luke 9:23

LEARNING TO DIE WELL

I'll never forget one day during my seminary days when I walked into Beeson Divinity School's bookstore and picked up a book on the history of world revivals. I remember that it was January, and the weather outside was awful. I even remember what I was wearing—which never happens to me. That day, I told a friend that I was going to hang out in the bookstore for a while, and then catch back up with him later. Later ended up being about six hours.

I picked up a book and read the story of William Seymour, and before long I was crying. William Seymour was an African-American pastor with Louisiana roots whom God moved to Los Angeles, California. William never saw revival coming. A humble nobody from nowhere, he was the son of a slave who became the point guard of the biggest outpouring move of God that the United States has ever seen. He was used by God to lead what became known as the Azusa Street Revival. All heaven broke loose on April 9, 1906, in William's small church in Los Angeles—including signs, wonders, healings, miracles, and people being baptized in the Spirit and filled with power. Azusa looked a lot like Pentecost in the book of Acts. The power of God was on full display. That January day, as I sat on the floor of the bookstore weeping, I said to God, "I want to be a part of seeing you move in unprecedented ways. Please, use me however you want to."

Revival was a theme of my seminary experience. During my first semester, I encountered a man who had a savage passion for revival. Dr. Lewis Drummond was in his 70s when I met him. His beloved students called him Lewie. People often joked that Dr. Drummond could lead an oak tree to Jesus Christ. The man never met a stranger, and he passionately talked about Jesus as though his very life depended upon it. Dr. Drummond taught a one-hour elective course on the Keswick Movement, and I decided to take it. To say that it stirred me up is an understatement. I was like a yellow jacket in an empty coke can. In this class, we studied some of the great moves of God over the years. When we talked about the move of God at Azusa, I became overwhelmed. I remember my right hand was shaking and I felt literal electricity flowing through my body. I was ready to run through a brick wall or two. Dr. Drummond looked at me one day and said, "Son, give Him all you have. Give Him all you have."

All these years later, I find myself even hungrier for revival than I was as a young man. I've seen a lot of people whose passion for Jesus and

His Kingdom wanes over the years. The opposite is happening to me. I never want my desire for God to decrease one ounce. At Bridgeway, we have no desire to play church. We are not interested in slick programs, church marketing, church growth strategies, catchy slogans, or any form of religiosity. We are going after awakening and asking Father for the wisdom and revelation on how to play any role that He has for us to help steward what He wants. We know we want to develop a culture of family, of community, a culture that honors the Word and the power of Holy Spirit. We want to be all in. We want to develop disciples like Jesus did. We have learned that all of these things require much of each one of us. We want our lives to look like Jesus, not eliminating anything. We want intimacy, connection with the Father—to wisely seek Him in all we do, obeying quickly, hearing Him, speaking His words, seeing His works on the earth, and making disciples as we go. The more that we lean into these things, the more God is showing us the power of consecration. In the end, no human has ever been able to control what God does or even how He does something. While this reality is true, our continued walk with God reveals that we do have complete control over two things: our consecration and our level of that consecration. Consecration means letting go, being willing to be free of anything that does not look like Jesus.

Luke 9:23 is a banner that Bridgeway sits under. We genuinely want to die well. We want to become less so that He can become more in us. When asked how Bridgeway has built a naturally supernatural culture, my answer is very simple. First, we have learned how to die over and over by consecrating our lives. Second, we have learned how to receive love from the Father and release that love to other people with the simple belief that God still wants to heal people, He still wants them walking in freedom, and He wants to build and encourage through prophecy.

HUNGER

I have noticed one common trait in every single place where God has poured Himself out over the years—people simply hunger for His presence in a way that could be considered extreme. I believe hunger is a gift and that it is also contagious. I also believe that many churches don't follow the ethos of Jesus. They choose to eliminate the works completely, cherry-picking which parts of the Word they want to follow. Jesus Christ focused on three things during His ministry here on earth—He taught the Kingdom, healed the sick, and delivered people of demons. In America, it's possible to have a successful ministry and not focus on any of those three things. Is this sincerely ok? I don't believe it is. We should desire His presence more than we desire our next breath. Many in church today do not know that there is a supernatural place they can tap into now. Others know, but they choose to walk away because when God's Spirit comes, things can get messy. At Bridgeway, I see a body of people yearn for the garment of Jesus Christ in the way the lady with the issue of blood did. I see people with a pure and simple desire to see Jesus pour Himself out the way He did when He walked the earth. Jesus hasn't changed—we have. Honestly, it's undeniable that hunger, especially corporate hunger, moves people to get into a position to receive extraordinary things from God. Hunger matters. People who want to walk in the works of the Father (John 10:38) need a level of aggressiveness. Until you want a culture at your church that is naturally supernatural more than you want your next breath, you'll probably never see it manifest.

Jesus lived a life of discipline. His ethos was to rise early. Many scholars believe that He spent three to four hours in prayer daily. He memorized the Torah. Was it boring? Or was it hunger? Both can bring breakthrough. If Jesus, fully God, deity, came to the earth and still needed hours daily with Papa, then why do we think we don't need the Word and times of seclusion. Building friendship with God includes making time and space for Him. What many people call extreme, God calls normal. Jesus was prepared by God for 30 years before He was released into public ministry. He worked a job. He was in a family. He studied. He prayed. He developed an ethos, a rhythm of discipline and of rest and solitude. During this time He grew in wisdom and revelation. At 30 years of age He had more intellectual knowledge than He did at 12 when He was found in His Father's house.

Is it extreme for someone living in today's world to read over 100 books a year about people who have been used greatly by God in the Kingdom? It all depends on what we call extreme. I believe leaders are hungry readers who want to learn from others. My love for reading biographies and historical accounts of the moves of God, even the ones that went wonky, has continued to increase my hunger for more of God. It is extraordinary to watch Father land on a group of people who have chosen to be led by hunger, not convenience. Every move of God starts with a group of hungry people. In Wales, before the Revival broke out in 1904, a group of young people were diligently reading the Word and spending time in prayer and worship, night and day. The sounds of worship that came from that period can still be heard in our modern worship songs. God goes to unlikely places like Nazareth, Los Angeles, Wales, Toronto, Redding, San Francisco, Brownsville, even Greenville, SC and He pours out His Spirit on the hungry, those who die to selfishness. Hunger and humility are a magnet for the Holy Spirit.

Our church decided that we simply could not go another day without seeing his Kingdom manifest so we got extreme. At that point in our history, Steve and Becky Keyes led our church. Becky decided to go to a conference in Virginia Beach with some other women of the church to investigate if Holy Spirit was still as real today as He was in the Bible. God had a surprise for her. What happened to Becky on that trip eventually spilled over into our church, because oil always flows from the top down. She came back completely refreshed and filled with the baptism of the

Holy Spirit. With Becky's encouragement, Steve decided to go all in with the Holy Spirit and lead our church in a different direction. Steve later said, "God showed me that this is what He wanted, so I said, 'OK.'"

We had no idea what we were in for. Our church was called Crossroads Community Church at the time. It was during this period that a remnant of people at this typical seeker-friendly church got completely fed up with a powerless form of Christianity. We had a firm foundation of the Word, great community, and a genuine love for Jesus at our church. Yet it was powerless Christianity. We never saw the power of the Holy Spirit like Jesus saw—specifically in the area of healings and deliverances and the prophetic. Our hunger positioned us for the stirring that was to come. Nobody wanted to pursue some weird tangent or chase some flippant theology. In all honesty, what disturbed us was what we found in the gospel of John and the book of Acts. We came to realize what many others have—that there comes a point when calling yourself a disciple of Jesus Christ is problematic if there is little to no evidence of the power of the Holy Spirit in operation in your life. Hunger set in.

TEACH THE KINGDOM, HEAL AND DELIVER

Being a disciple of Jesus Christ means seeing power in operation regularly, like we see with Jesus' disciples. I believe that what many people call discipleship in the Western church is actually consulting. There's nothing wrong with consulting, it's just not discipleship. Paul said that the Kingdom of God is not a matter of talk but of power (1 Corinthians 4:20). Discipleship means being as interested in the Father's works as Jesus was. Healings and deliverances were not a subsidiary part of the ministry of Christ, and should not be for us, either. At some point, we need to face our own inadequacies with this aspect of discipleship with vulnerability and courage instead of running from the conversation and building theologies and methodologies around things and ideas that oppose who Jesus is and what He taught.

Around 2002, about 20 of us at Crossroads began to read the gospels and the book of Acts seriously and expectantly. Things began to heat up as we prayed and read the Scriptures. A small group of people decided to start a prayer ministry. The ministry was always under the authority of Steve and Becky and the Elders. It was not a renegade group trying to hijack the church. It began as intercession, then people started showing up asking for prayer. Listening then speaking only what the Father was sharing through the Word and Spirit became our methodology, and it remains so. At the beginning, I thought this would bring the church together—that people would actually be excited about Holy Spirit breaking out in power in our church. I was genuinely naïve because I believed that people would become really excited as our church took seriously the three things Jesus did: teaching the Kingdom, healing, and deliverance. I could not have been more wrong.

It's a misconception to think that a group of people going after the Lord in this way will result in unity, peace, and harmony. From my experience, and from the historic stories I read, it's far more likely for brothers to become divided and for believers to go separate ways because they can't agree on the theology of revival, or the methodology of doing what Jesus did. Take Azusa Street as an example. Over 6 million lives were deeply impacted, and the Gospel literally went all over the world. Yet it is undeniable that even that church was incredibly divided on the person of the Holy Spirit and the manifestations that accompanied that great movement.

I love the idea of unity, and I pray for it regularly, but I do not ignore the trend in the history of the Kingdom of God that when the Holy Spirit shows up in power, it tends to divide instead of unite. Perhaps Jesus was onto something when He said, "I did not come to bring peace, but a sword" (Matthew 10:34). When I look back at the history of the church, I can't help but notice that the Holy Spirit does not mind leading people who are in love with Him straight into conflict. I have often pondered this in order to understand it, and I have come to believe that to God, conflict is not a bad thing at all. Conflict actually reveals what is inside us. I believe the enemy leaves many churches alone because they are not much of a threat to his kingdom. I can promise you that if, under the grace of God, you get a culture up and running that sees the Father's works manifest, you are sure to bump into the enemy often. If you want to build a naturally supernatural culture at your church or in your community, you should start with a sober and honest reflection of whether you truly desire this. Counting the cost is wise and necessary.

When I decided that I would rather walk with God—doing the things that His Son did while He was here—than call myself a pastor and not do two of the three things Jesus did while He was in ministry—I had a strong hunch of what it would cost me. Even so, I said yes. I believe a strong, measurable indicator of our relationships with God is obedience. When God cracked the door to the prophetic for me, I peeked in and said, "Yes, I want this no matter what." Now my passion is to help churches and pastors who are skeptical learn how to open that door. I want to help turn their influence into something that resembles what Jesus did while He was here. Most of the battle is about deciding up front that the cost is worth it. If we will take a baby step toward the things that God is passionate about, then He will scoop us up and help us more than we could ever imagine as we go about building naturally supernatural cultures. He cracks the door and invites us to step in. Once we step in, the ball starts rolling. Once the ball starts rolling, the enemy begins to have an "uh oh" moment. I believe that it is time for the enemy to have a lot of "uh oh" moments. I desire to give my life to see normal churches full of normal people begin to believe and understand that God will use any of us to build these naturally supernatural cultures wherever we are. He wants us to know that it can be fun, exciting, and a great learning experience. There is nothing like praying for someone who has some incurable situation and watching God help that person.

Our church lost around 35 families when Steve decided to preach on the Holy Spirit. Many people believed that we would become crazy and drift away from sound doctrine. I get it, because I used to be one of those people. Even five years after my encounter with Jesus, I didn't want to talk about it. I didn't want people to think I was crazy. Honestly, I cared more about what people thought than I did about what God was doing with me. I looked around one day at church and thought, "Well, we may lose everyone." Yet, I had never felt more alive in my life than I did in that season. I felt like I was on the frontier of undiscovered territory and it excited me to no end. We had gold dust manifesting, oil appearing in hands, wind blowing in rooms, rooms filling up with the smell of heaven, blind eyes seeing, deaf ears opening, and many other wonderful healings. Yet while all of this was happening people were leaving.

WORD AND SPIRIT

At the time that the Kingdom of God was breaking out at Crossroads, I was serving as an itinerant minister and a co-founder of Wayfarer Ministries. I preached at youth camps and conferences, wrote curriculum for churches, and served on the preaching team at Crossroads while all this Holy Spirit activity manifested. I was simply excited about seeing the things that Jesus saw. In the early days, I got so excited when I saw someone healed that I could barely stand it. I grew up with the view that God was a mean and distant person, and now I was watching Him heal people, sometimes quite dramatically. I'm still not over it all these years later. He is amazing, and I can't wait to see Him one day. He is the nicest person I've ever met in my life. As a matter of fact, when you begin to realize how nice He is and start seeing people healed left and right, you will not care much about the people who come against you. When you have the revelation in your heart that the God of the universe has a picture of you in His wallet, nothing else ruffles your feathers like it used to.

After a few years, God called me to join the staff of Crossroads Community Church as a discipleship pastor. I went through another major crisis, this time not of identity, or sonship, or the supernatural. This time I was slammed in the face with the recognition that we in the Western church do a lot of work *for* God, but we don't do a lot of work *with* God. We have programs that benefit people, but we do not disciple them in the naturally supernatural ways of Jesus. We tend not to introduce them to Father and to their place at the Table. My crisis involved not just me building my own deep friendship with Father, or me learning to step out in faith and heal the sick, or me growing in the gift of prophecy. The questions that I began asking myself were, "Am I making disciples? Am I bringing others to the Table? And am I helping them to develop into disciples in all the ways of Jesus. If I love God, am I loving others enough to invite them in?"

Crossroads Community Church went through many major changes. There was a change in leadership, and a name change to City Church. In my previous book, *Signs, Wonders and a Baptist Preacher*, I discuss City Church and many of the great ministries established there. It was in transition from being a Word church to becoming a Word and Spirit church. Steve Keyes had moved on to another assignment. As I was busy on my personal journey of discovering what true discipleship means, the lead pastor who had taken over for Steve resigned. Growing up, I had told God that I loved Him very much but I did not want to be a pastor. I have always enjoyed traveling and speaking and meeting new people. That was my comfort zone. The thought of being in one place pastoring seemed like a nightmare to me. Most pastors I knew stayed exhausted and were not the happiest people in the world. Well, God has His plans. When the elders offered me the job, I said, "OK, let's give it a go." I had zero experience in pastoring a church. I had been preaching for twenty years, but we all know that is only a small part of pastoring. In my first meeting with the elders I said, "I probably should not say this at my first meeting, but God told me that we will be moving soon." There was an awkward pause, and then we laughed a little. One of the elders asked, "Where are we moving?" I said, "I have no clue." How many of you know that the Promised Land becomes visible as we walk?

Shortly after that, God gave Steve Keyes (who remains on staff with us) a dream that I was pastoring a church in our town called Mt. Zion Fellowship. I looked right at Steve and said, "Who is in charge at Mt. Zion?" I knew in that moment that God was merging two churches: City Church and Mt. Zion Christian Fellowship. Mt. Zion's pastor had recently resigned. They had 40 acres of land and a building, but no pastor. The church's core had dwindled to around 50-75 people. In a room that seats 500, this crowd seemed quite small. With another pastor from our church, I drove over to meet with Jack and Amonda Hancock. This couple in their 70s had helped found Mt. Zion Fellowship over 30 years earlier. Mt. Zion started as a Bible study in their home in the 1970's. The Hancocks have a history in Spirit-filled living. Amonda's dad was actually a traveling healing evangelist back during the heyday of the healing movement in the 1950s. When we met with the Hancocks, we knew that God was up to something. We both sensed very quickly that God was calling us to merge churches. We had people and needed to expand, and Mt. Zion had a building that needed people. We both had the common vision of wanting to help people build deep friendship with God and one another.

I can't tell you how many people warned me against merging churches. I heard every horror story you can imagine about the dangers of merging. Yet, as I heard reservations from others, God kept telling me that the merger would be like a hot knife through warm butter. His grace was all over this merge. When God gives you an assignment, He makes a way. I cast vision for both elder boards and said, "We will be called Bridgeway Church. We will be a church that stands in the radical middle of the Word and Spirit. We will be a church that is passionate about being naturally supernatural." I told the elders of my long-term plan to build a healthy environment of discipleship where we train people how to live in the ways of the Kingdom while operating under a strong revelation of the Word itself.

I've noticed over the years that there seems to have been a divorce in the church between the Spirit and the Word. I wanted to pastor a church that honored both. In the years since the merge, we realize that we are watching that dream turn into a reality. Bridgeway is becoming solidified as a church that takes His Word seriously and that is also passionate about operating with Holy Spirit and being open to all of His works. If we go too long around here without a story of miraculous breakthrough, we get antsy. We want to honor the places and people of the past who saw God do impossible things, but we are tired of just reading old stories. We want God to show off here. We want to see incurable diseases healed and people set free constantly. It's not because we read some person's book on charismatic theology. We desire this because we find Jesus, in the gospels, passionate about these same things. Healing is not our idea—it has always been God's idea.

OBEDIENCE

I am convinced that what we call processing, God calls disobedience. There are times in your assignment when He gives you a window of opportunity to respond and then moves on to the next person. You can literally lose your assignment by not being willing to say yes, then do your work as to the Lord. He will test you to see just how far He can stretch you. He may even give you assignments that seem ridiculous. Just as I like to reward my children when they do something and do it well, so our heavenly Father likes to encourage and bless our obedience. I have done some crazy things in obedience to God, even things I said I would never do, like pastor a church. God spoke to me one day and said, "Son, I want you to fly to Azusa Street, lick the ground, and fly back to Bridgeway Church and spit on the ground three times." For a guy who grew up in a Baptist church, I sure have come a long way, I guess. So, I got on a plane and flew to Los Angeles to the famous site of the great outpouring of God that started on April 9, 1906, when heaven broke loose in the City of Angels—Los Angeles, California. As I sat on a bench and looked around, I reflected on why God had me fly out to Los Angeles to be at Azusa. The place where the church was located is now an office complex area with only a few plaques that remind people of what happened in downtown Los Angeles. I did not have any goose bumps or deep spiritual revelations as I sat there. I was mostly so incredibly grateful for Pastor Seymour, his wife Jenny, and the people who led that move of God for so many years. I thanked God for their lives and impact, and then I prayed two things. First, I asked the Father to literally guide me to where the front of the church was 110 years ago. Second, I asked Him to use Bridgeway Church in Greenville, South Carolina, to help a lot of people find what people found at Azusa more than 100 years ago.

Ten minutes after I prayed, I sensed the Holy Spirit wanted me to walk toward a specific part of the office complex. As I walked, I stopped and knew that I was standing in a very important place. With a security guard looking on, I got down on my knees, licked the ground of one of the most important places in American church history, and said, "God, I'm all yours. Use me however You want. I really want to know You as a friend." Then, I flew back to Greenville. Soon after I arrived home, I got down on my knees in the middle of the property of Bridgeway Church and spit three times. No angels, no thunder from the sky, and no deep revelations happened. I simply knew that I was being obedient to what the Father wanted me to do. I've learned a few simple things in my years on this earth. One of them is that I can't control what God will do, but I can always control my level of obedience to what He is calling me and my family to do. I don't know why I was supposed to lick Azusa Street and spit on Bridgeway's campus, but I obeyed. Maybe someday I will have more revelation.

On this team and in this family we simply want one thing: we want to see God move powerfully. This is not a trite little saying to us. We sincerely desire awakening, and we are asking God to start with us. I think back to the day when I cried when reading the story of Azusa. The passion I had that day is the passion I have now. I want to see God move in unprecedented ways in my life and sphere of influence. I have no desire to play church. I want to see God do the things through us that He did through Jesus. John 14:12 has to be true. We as a team have counted the cost and are comfortable with whatever comes our way. He's worth it even though pursuing this is a guarantee that the waters will get choppy.

CHOPPY WATERS

Our church has experienced growth, but in the early years it wasn't this way at all. We lost members. It is a misconception to think that, if you pursue a naturally supernatural culture through sound teaching and calm methodology, your church will automatically grow. You may actually experience the opposite. As you count the cost, it is wise to step into these waters out of obedience and a desire to be faithful to the command of the Lord for His disciples to heal the sick. (See Matthew 10:8) Don't try to build this kind of culture as some kind of church growth strategy. When you're in the water of obedience and hit a choppy stretch, you will have so much confidence that you are rowing in the direction the Lord wants you to row that you will move forward confidently, no matter what others say or do. You will be able to abide in Him and remain obedient, regardless of what is happening around you.

Too many churches care more about being financially stable and culturally relevant than about John 14:12 breaking out in their midst. I had a conversation with a megachurch pastor on this very topic. He was very interested in developing a naturally supernatural culture at his church, but ultimately decided against it because it simply was not worth it to him. He believed it would be too divisive and cause too many distractions. In many ways, I don't blame this man. He has laid his life down for the church he is pastoring, and God is doing many great things there. People are blessed at the church he pastors, and he loves the Lord with all of his heart. This pastor knows that people would likely leave left and right if they started a healing ministry and out-of-the-box things started to happen. He counted the cost and decided against it. Personally, I don't think he will end up on the junior varsity team in heaven or fail to experience the favor of the Lord on his life. I think he counted the cost and made the decision to protect what God is doing in the church instead of rocking the boat to a place that would cause perceived distraction.

In the beginning stages of our church's transition, we were hungry enough and courageous enough to count the cost and decide it was worth it. I thought we would lose ten families max. I had no idea that so many people would leave. They did—but we have survived, and now we're thriving. It was the right decision because it was the culture God wanted us to create. When I talk to pastors, I share these very practical steps on how to wisely move forward into becoming a naturally supernatural church.

1. Oil flows from the top down in the Kingdom. Unless the senior pastor is 100 percent on board, there is too big a risk of dishonor being in play in your church or ministry.

2. Develop your paradigm for healing and deliverance ministry from the Word itself, and not from other author's books or pastor's teachings. Rely on the Word of God, not anyone else's word exclusively.

3. Make sure you are committed to a culture of development and not of delivery. This will ensure that supernatural ministry is

about training others to do the works of the Father, so it does not rest on the shoulders of one or a few. In the old days, people traveled great distances to get near a great man or woman of God to receive a touch of heaven. I believe the current days are about common and ordinary people learning how to operate in the gifts of the spirit. A culture of development is far more practical than a culture of delivery. Jesus could have built a mega ministry based on His mass healings crusades, but instead He continued to take time away from the crowds so He could develop those around Him to do the works of the Father. Jesus was constantly working Himself out of a job.

4. Develop a clear and simple plan to train people in the supernatural (including healing, deliverance, and prophetic words) that you can play out in training courses, in church-wide events, and in core groups or other forms of organized communities and groups at your church.

When people come to Bridgeway to learn how to build a naturally supernatural culture at their church, they quickly discover that we are not geniuses. I don't even let people call me pastor. Just call me by my name. My seminary degree does not hang on my wall, and I don't have God figured out. What we can offer others is many years of learning what to and what not to do. We have journeyed through the choppy waters of turning a normal seeker-friendly church in the Willow Creek model into a church that has a sustainable ethos of breakthrough for people in an environment that has not forsaken the Word or sound doctrine. I know it's possible because I've seen it happen here. We've journeyed from Crossroads to City Church and Mt. Zion and now to Bridgeway. We are built by the Father to be a place that can share with common pastors from all over the world what it looks like to take the works of the Father seriously. There is nothing like seeing someone in the Kingdom who thinks that the works are only for the super saints, come to find out that they are for everyone. I tell people all of the time that if God can use me as a pastor, then anybody has a fighting chance. I sincerely pray that people will count the cost, get the training, and persevere to see a supernatural culture established at their place of influence. He's worth it.

We lie if we tell people this is easy. Not everyone will go to the extremes of radical obedience. Not everyone will fly across the country to lick a sidewalk. You may call it extreme. I call it obedience. He uses the foolish to confound the wise. Some will stay in the land of coziness, knowing about God, but never developing into a disciple. Some will learn all they can, and see great miracles and signs and wonders while growing a huge ministry without ever discipling others to do the same. A true Son goes first then pulls others forward. One of the things I love most about our church is that we have developed a culture of constantly training and equipping people to do the works of Father while building friendship with Him and one another. We are not perfect. But we at least take the risk. Sometimes messy is worth it. The testimonies of the people who come through here and can say with absolute surety that they were healed, set free, encouraged and loved by our people—that's worth the cost, every day, all the time.

For Bridgeway, we counted the cost and decided that it was worth it to take John 14:12 seriously. For us it was worth it to not despise prophecy and all of the other gifts. May you find the courage to be more like Jesus than so many of the models of ministry that play it safe. Jesus focused on teaching the Kingdom, healing the sick, and delivering people of the enemy. You can have a successful church in the West and not even glance at the three things Jesus focused on. May you simply not be OK with that paradigm in your life. In the name of Jesus Christ, I bless you with the courage to move forward with His paradigm as yours. May you do this no matter what it costs you.

Chapter 12

GRATITUDE

MY THREE CHILDREN could not be more different from each other. Sam, Ruthie, and Jack are fun kids to be around and I can honestly say that my wife and I enjoy all three in three different ways. Sam is the responsible older brother who could probably run for public office in our city and win at the age of 14. Ruthie is the ultimate teacher who is always helping her little brother Jack improve in every area of his life on a consistent basis. At 11, Ruthie is showing signs of being the identical twin of her mother. Jack is like Mowgli from *The Jungle Book*. He is wild in his heart and lives with a passion that is contagious. At 8, Jack teaches us to never grow up no matter how old we become. Over the last few years, I have noticed something with my three children that has gotten my attention and taught me a lot about the Kingdom of God as it relates to building deep friendship with God. When my kids tell me "Thank you" after I have provided them with a meal, gift, or trip of some sort, it sincerely makes me want to give them even more. When they are acting selfish and fail to express thanks to me or their mom, it actually bothers us, quenching our heart's desire to give more.

We have so greatly underestimated the power of gratitude. I believe gratitude is the number one weapon in the Kingdom. Psalm 100:4 says that we are to enter His courts with thanksgiving. Have you ever given serious thought to the benefits of genuine thanksgiving? A few years ago God began to show me the power of gratitude. I have seen God move in my life from victory to victory without me even praying for breakthrough. This has happened over and over again. As a matter of fact, He began to give me revelation on how He fights battles on our behalf that we are not even aware of when we are walking in true gratitude. One night I was struggling with a decision that I needed to make in leadership and I said, "Father, I cannot discern what it is that you want me to do." He said, "Worship me and you will know what to do." The Father loves gratitude. He loves thanksgiving. He is not drawn to a critical spirit. Gratitude is a hallmark of spiritual maturity. The highest form of spiritual warfare is genuine thankfulness before God, because He will defeat your enemies for you if you just remain thankful. He will defeat enemies you don't even know you have. Why would you enter His courts with bickering and complaining? Why would you spend time reminding God of what He hasn't done for you? A high form of wisdom asks, "Do I walk out gratitude, or am I more known for bickering about the manna?"

I had a dream one night that I was in my dad's basement, where a good friend and I started Wayfarer Ministries. In this dream two young women from the church were there, along with their two kids, who were playing. I walked to my left and I was in Bridgeway's building. There were 2,500 people in the church. There were 2,500 more seats behind the church, and they filled up very fast. I headed back to my basement and walked to the back of the room. My dad was there working at a desk and the two young women and their kids were still there as well. But here's the most unexpected thing—there was a terrorist in the closet. He looked at me. I looked back at him and I was not scared of him. I walked toward him, and he started backing up. I asked him, "What are you doing here?" He did not answer. I walked back into the room and the terrorist was getting annoyed and fidgety. It happened a third time, and I saw a mass of computer terminals in the closet. Then, the terrorist left to go back to his homeland. On the computer terminals, I watched his own community of people, his brotherhood, kill him. I got an interpretation from the Father in the middle the dream. He said, "Chad, if you will remain thankful, gratitude will be your biggest weapon. I will turn your enemies against themselves all the days of your life."

We don't wrestle against flesh and blood. If you're bumping into someone who is grumbling and engaging in divisive issues or behaviors, they may not even know that they're being used by the enemy to stir up conflict. I'm not talking about people outside of Christ. You can pray in tongues and walk in no character, and be used by the enemy worse than someone who does not know the Lord. In my dream, God was saying, "Don't ever harp too much on strategy. Don't try to figure this thing out. Just be like Jehoshaphat. Put the worshipers in front. Put the people full of gratitude in front and I'll do the rest."

What I want to explain through Scripture is this—when we thank Him from the Table, it's not just for Him to say "Oh, you're welcome." Thankfulness actually releases the angelic realm into our lives; it releases breakthrough. Thankfulness actually wars against the enemy. Let me say it this way—when one of my kids tells me, "Hey dad, I just wanted to say thank you," it actually makes me want to multiply what I've already given them and give them more.

TUGGING ON HIS GRACE

A strong indicator of a true son or daughter sitting at the King's Table is they just can't stop thanking Him. They're always telling Him: "You are so good. You're so good. You're just so good." This is thanksgiving coming from a pure heart, with no desire to manipulate God. It comes from a pure place of gratitude and can open doors you never even thought to intercede for. What if you just start being thankful and then ten years from now, you turn around and say, "How did so much favor flow in my life?" What if it's because of two things: God is good, and you tugged on that grace with your faith and genuine thanksgiving? For example, a lot of people get tripped up on finances, because they do not bring their firstfruits to the Father and present them at their local church. When you bring your firstfruits and offer them to Father, it is more than just words. Your firstfruits are an offering of thanksgiving. Spiritual orphans say, "God, I've been disappointed in you for so long in my life. It is all about me and You never come through for me. I'm in Christ, thank goodness for heaven. I guess I'll see you there whenever." Spiritual sons and daughters say, "Father, you're too good, you're just good. Thank you so much. If you never did another thing for me, I've got it pretty good. When I leave my body, I'm going to be with you forever. This is too good to be true. You are awesome. You are awesome, God."

One night when I was preaching in Tennessee, I told God, "You are incredible." He replied, "I think you are incredible too." When we act like Him, it thrills Him and even brings rewards that perhaps we have not considered. The things that look like heaven manifest in our lives because of gratitude. These things show up in our marriage, with our kids, with our finances, and with our protection. They're all ushered in by saying, "I want to say thank You."

OUT OF THE MOUTH THE HEART SPEAKS

Gratitude is one of the major themes of the Bible.

> *"Give thanks in all circumstances; for this is God's will for you in Christ Jesus."*
>
> 1 Thessalonians 5:18

> *"Do not be anxious about anything, but in every situation, by prayer and petition, with thanksgiving, present your requests to God."*
>
> Philippians 4:6

Isn't it interesting that you thank Him, *then* you request? If you are requesting without gratitude as a staple in your life, you might as well hush because you are wasting your breath. This is why He said things like, "Bring Me the firstfruits" and "Anoint your first born." When you know the nature of someone, you can always predict their behavior. Father loves the firstfruits of anything, including gratitude and thankfulness. We say, "thank you" as a quick blessing before our meals, but sincere, heartfelt gratitude is so much more than that. Thankfulness is saying from the heart, "You are so good."

God's Word is constantly reminding us to give Him thanks.

> *"Give thanks to the LORD, for He is good; His love endures forever."*
>
> Psalm 107:1

> *"I'll give thanks to the Lord because of his righteousness; I will sing the praises of the name of the LORD Most High."*
>
> Psalm 7:17

> *"Always giving thanks to God the Father for everything, in the name of our Lord Jesus Christ."*
>
> Ephesians 5:20

Why is the Bible always reminding us to give thanks to Him? Because thanks produces genuine humility. Saying "thank you" every day reminds us that we didn't bring ourselves into this world. We came from Him. Everything is about Him. He deserves all my praise. I come to Him just because I'm thankful, not because I'm looking for Him to give me more things. Humility is not self-deprecation, it is recognition of His greatness. It is recognition of Him. Am I going to chase God for a platform? No. I am going to chase after a close seat at the King's Table because He's just good. I want to be as close to Him as possible. I want to be like the disciple John. I want to lean into His chest. I want to be so close it makes angels nervous. Honestly, we should be so close to Him that we are triggering the religious spirit every single day. I don't want to just be in the vine. I want to be deep in the vine. My body is decaying every single day, but there's never been anything decayed about Him. He's always existed. No one made Him. He told the sun, "You will be that big. You will be this hot, and I'm going to cause you to rise every single morning. I will make the moon my footstool—I am going to prop my feet up on it." He is Lord God Almighty, Jehovah. Every once in a while, we ought to say, "You are big. Thank You for being You." If you don't think you have anything else for which to thank Him, then at least thank Him for Jesus. Jesus was His firstfruits given to you.

> *"Shout for joy to the LORD, all the earth.*
> *Worship the LORD with gladness; come before him with joyful*
> *songs."*
>
> *Psalm 100:1-2*

Why are we to shout for joy to the Lord with gladness and joyful songs? Because He deserves it? Absolutely. And, not just because He deserves it. Our praise activates the things of heaven. It activates protection, deliverance, blessing on your marriage, blessing on your finances, and blessing on our job. If we would just stop griping and complaining about what we don't have and the prophetic word that didn't come to pass, stop acting like a little baby sucking our thumb, thinking, "nothing ever goes right for me," maybe we would see this activation. Nothing, beside offense, shows orphanhood more than a lack of gratitude. We shut the doors of heaven over us all the time by what comes out of our mouths. We are literally damming ourselves—damming up heaven's flow by being hypercritical all the time about ourselves and about what's not happening. Sometimes you just need to go before Him and your intercession simply needs be, "I just want to thank you." Over the next week, write down everything in your life you've ever been thankful for then watch what happens in you. I dare you.

THE WIND OF HEAVEN

I was pulling into my driveway one day and just started to tear up with thankfulness for everything God had done in my life, everything He had given me—my wife, my children, my house, His Son, and the reality that I get to spend all eternity with Him. Have you ever stopped to really think about that? We are prone to think that He loves other people more than He loves us. That is not true. He doesn't play favorites. You have a lot to be thankful for, if you will just realize it's all about Him and His goodness. This will happen when you sit at the King's Table. When we don't have gratitude, we believe "It's all about me. I deserve more than this. I deserve better." The truth is, we deserve hell. We don't deserve anything more. We don't deserve the breath in our bodies. When we are able to embrace that truth, we will start seeing with the eyes of an owl, a hawk, or an eagle. We will notice things to be thankful for, things other people don't notice. I am not saying we should thank Him in order to manipulate Him. He is brilliant, so that will not work. When you begin to genuinely thank Him out of pure gratitude, you will start to feel the wind of heaven, the downdraft of His blessings. Your gratitude will usher in the favor of God.

Don't allow yourself to become so weighted down by Lazarus' grave clothes that you can't see what to be thankful for. Take the grave clothes off and get out of Lo-debar. Don't search for someone else to pray for you, for someone else to lift the grave clothes off of you or to give you a lift out of Lo-debar. Take them off yourself. Some things are your responsibility, not God's, and not your community's. Develop the perspective of being thankful even in the most difficult of times. Jesus once had thousands of people to feed with only a little bit of bread and fish. The first thing He did was to give thanks to the Father. Then He turned around with enough food to feed thousands of people. Thankfulness positions us for the wind of heaven, the downdraft of His blessings. It's a pattern Jesus demonstrated for life in the Kingdom. We can go through life so unaware. If we could get a glimpse of all the things He has saved us from, we would cry and spend most of our days saying, "Thank You, thank You, thank You."

Imagine if you thanked Him and He replied, "No, thank *you*"? You see, when gratitude is pure, it tugs on the heart of the Father. He'll give you so much blessing you won't know what to do with it. We live in lack when our heart lacks thankfulness. If you struggle with thankfulness, go to His Word, find the places He talks of thankfulness and let them start to sink into your heart. "Know that the LORD is God. It is he who made us, and we are his; we are his people, the sheep of his pasture. Enter his gates with thanksgiving and his courts with praise; give thanks to him and praise his name" (Psalm 100:3-4).

RIDICULOUS GRATITUDE

The most ridiculous story on the power of gratitude that I can find in the New Testament is in Acts 16:16–40. Paul and Silas were beaten so badly that many scholars believe they probably suffered major swelling all over their bodies. Let's examine what got them into trouble and what they did afterward. "Once when we were going to the place of prayer, we were met by a female slave who had a spirit by which she predicted the future. She earned a great deal of money for her owners by fortune-telling. She followed Paul and the rest of us, shouting, "These men are servants of the Most High God, who are telling you the way to be saved." She kept this up for many days. Finally Paul became so annoyed that he turned around and said to the spirit, "In the name of Jesus Christ I command you to come out of her!" At that moment the spirit left her" (Acts 16:16-18). I love that Paul put up with this annoyance as long as he could. Then, he turned around and spoke to the spirit. He didn't speak to the lady, he spoke to the spirit. This is important. Often times what's coming against you is not flesh and blood, it's a spirit. If you treat the problem as though it's a person, that problem is going to get worse. Instead, take authority over what's behind that person. Watch what happened when Paul did this very thing. "In the name of Jesus Christ, I command you to come out of her. At that moment, the spirit left her." It left her *at that moment*. Funny how that works.

The crowd then joined in the attack against Paul and Silas. "When her owners realized that their hope of making money was gone, they seized Paul and Silas and dragged them into the marketplace to face the authorities. They brought them before the magistrates and said, 'These men are Jews, and are throwing our city into an uproar by advocating customs unlawful for us Romans to accept or practice'" (Acts 16:19-21). All things seemed to be against them at that point. The magistrate ordered them to be stripped and beaten with rods. It was pretty intense. After they had been severely flogged, they were thrown into prison and the jailer was commanded to guard them carefully. What would you do if this happened to you? A spiritual orphan would bicker and complain. A spiritual son would remain in a posture of gratitude.

After they were beaten, Paul and Silas were put in an inner cell, the deepest part of the prison. "Upon receiving such orders, he put them in the inner cell and fastened their feet in the stocks" (Acts 16:24). If ever an orphan spirit could have manifested, that was the time. So, what did Paul do? "About midnight Paul and Silas were praying and singing hymns to God, and the other prisoners were listening to them. Suddenly there was such a violent earthquake that the foundations of the prison were shaken. At once all the prison doors flew open, and everybody's chains came loose" (Acts 16:25-26). Their praise became a weapon that set them free! When you are so deep at the King's Table, suffering and persecution don't seem the same to you as they do to a spiritual orphan because you know you don't deserve anything in the first place.

Sometimes we treat thankfulness like it's just a sweet sentiment, but it is so much more. The reason many of us don't walk in freedom is because we don't walk in gratitude. Every gift you have is from the Father of Lights. This is why Paul says he learned to be content in all things. He was content when he was being beaten and when he was not being beaten. He was so connected to God that he could just say, "You know what, if this is the end for me, it's been a good ride. I will be with You forever anyway." If I get to the end of my life and I am petrified and I'm trying to hang onto the earth because I don't want to go, that tells me something. It tells me that I may believe in Him, but I don't really know Him. This is why—when you really know Him, even the end your life is no big deal. You can say, "Hey, if it ends right here today, I'm going to be with You forever." If you never had another breakthrough in your life, you still have a pretty great ending to the story. Every once in a while, a person just grows up and realizes they don't have to get their identity from their kids or their spouse or their parents or their job. They can be so connected to the Father that if things never changed, they know they've got it pretty good.

Louis Armstrong was right—it is a wonderful world, but you've got to see it for what it is. Paul and Silas did. They were tied up, yet saying, "What a wonderful God, what a wonderful world!" Then, all of a sudden—BAM! Chains were loosed and they could go free. But did they? If that had happened to a bunch of charismatics, many of them would run around yelling, "I'm out of my prison! I got what I asked for! I'm out of my prison! I got what I asked for! There's my breakthrough! I sowed my seed, and got my breakthrough." But that's not what Paul and Silas did. They just kept singing. The jailer woke up, and when he saw the prison doors open, he drew his sword to kill himself because he thought the prisoners had escaped. Paul shouted, "Don't harm yourself, we're all here." The jailer called for lights, rushed in, and fell trembling before Paul and Silas. Gratitude is powerful. People tremble at a person of deep gratitude. Pray for the courage to be a person of gratitude.

When you have deep friendship with God, the enemy trembles. The praise of Paul and Silas drew others to the God they were worshipping, causing the jailer to ask them, "What must I do to be saved?" (Acts 16:30). Their reply—"Believe in the Lord Jesus, and you will be saved, you and your household." Then they spoke the word of the Lord to him and to all the others in his house. At that hour of the night the jailer took them and washed their wounds; then immediately he and all his household were baptized. The jailer brought them into his house and set a meal before them; he was filled with joy because he had come to believe in God—he and his whole household. When it was daylight the magistrates sent their officers to the jailer with the order: "Release those men" (Acts 16:31-35). I can imagine Paul saying, "I've already been released. You don't need to release me. I wasn't really bound up in the first place."

Jesus could have called down legions of angels when He was on that cross. He was tied up and accused of a crime He didn't commit, but even then, He kept his mouth shut. Why? Because His identity was determined at the King's Table, not by what was around Him. Jesus had the authority to walk right out of there, but He didn't. Instead, He embraced the cross because that was His assignment. When you are at the King's Table, prison seasons will come and go and some may even come directly from the hand of the Father to groom you more in the image of Jesus Christ. You trust Him in and out of the prison seasons.

I'm afraid much of the church has little understanding of this message of suffering. When the Father sends you into a tough season, both of you will see what you are made of. Paul is called the greatest overcomer of all time, other than Jesus Christ by most biblical historians. Some of you reading this book have tremendous destinies in your future. In order to get there you have to overcome whatever is standing in your way. It's easy to thank Him when things are flowing. However, if you can't thank Him from the prison cell, when the doubts are invading and things aren't going your way, then the concept of gratitude might not yet be fully real to you. Learn to thank Him from prison, when your faith waivers, when you cannot feel His presence, in the midst of your pain. Thank Him just because you're so thankful you can't help yourself.

Many churches blow up numerically because the people are thinking, "If I learn a certain theology, or practice a new methodology and think a certain way, then His blessing has to be mine." That's a religious spirit. God wants relationship, not religion. When you're in relationship with the Father and the blessings are manifesting, you're not running out to touch them, you are not grabbing them, you are not tweeting about how blessed you are. You would rather just stay at the King's Table and thank Him. Because you have learned to be content in all things— when blessings are tangible and when they are not. You have come to understand that it's not all about you. You become a laid down lover. God loves to pick up laid down lovers and give them resurrection power so that no prison cell can contain them. It was inappropriate for the officials to say to Paul, "Now you can be released." He was released when Jesus blinded his eyes on the road to Emmaus. Paul's freedom led him to a life of thankfulness at the King's Table.

If you're not a person of extreme gratitude, you probably don't know what you should be thankful for. Try meditating on the thought that, if not for Jesus Christ, you would rot and spend eternity in hell. I don't know about you, but I'm thankful that is not my future. I'm thankful I get to be reunited with family members. I'm thankful that I have a wife who loves Jesus and goes after Him. I'm thankful that I have three kids who go after the Lord. I'm thankful for my church. I am thankful that I have water to drink. I'm thankful I was raised by parents who love God. I'm thankful for my siblings. I'm thankful that there was money for me to go to my dream school, the University of Georgia. I'm thankful we have carpet. I'm thankful that if it rains, we have a roof that keeps us from getting wet. I'm thankful that we have a place to come worship the Father. I can keep going, but I will just tell you one thing: if this kind of thankfulness is not natural for you, it doesn't make you evil. It probably means that you are still wearing Lazarus's grave clothes. Learn what it means to live to be thankful. Let praise continually be on your lips. When we are thankful, other people want to be around us. Our thankfulness draws others to us and to Him. I read an article three years ago about why people get promoted in the workplace. It's called "the likability factor." It's not competency, or character, it's chemistry. It's the likability factor that gets people promoted. Heaven's agenda is drawn to people who are thankful. You may need to thank someone in your life right now, just for being who they are. Simple gratitude goes a long way. It makes sons out of orphans.

Chapter 13

JOY

I **LOVE TO ASK GOD A LOT OF QUESTIONS.** I asked Him one
day, "What am I going to do when I first get to heaven?" He replied,
"Chad, you are going to have the biggest feast you have ever had in
your life. You will also learn how to cook. You've always wanted to be
a fantastic cook." I'm sure that His answer will make many eyes roll
because it's not serious enough for many people who follow God. I can't
say that this is what I was expecting Him to say. If you would have asked
me what His answer would have been, I probably would have leaned
more to the side of, "You will learn to worship me forever and continue
to grow in revelation of my greatness throughout all time." Although

I'm sure that those two things will happen when I'm up there, that is not what He told me. I think some of us are too serious and tightly wound to hear God on an ongoing basis. Some of us associate God with nothing but a heaviness and seriousness, perhaps forgetting that He is also our Father. If the Lord Jesus' yoke is easy and His burden is light, then that is the way His Father and our Father is wired as well.

I believe with all of my heart that seriousness is not a fruit of the spirit. In fact, God has shown me that this is a key to walking in a deep level of the prophetic. There have been people leave Bridgeway because they are so serious about seriousness that anything else is offensive. As for me, I care more about understanding His character and nature than anything in the world. When I heard Him tell me that I would learn to cook, I shook my head. It blows my mind that as huge as He is, He also has a side to Him that simply wants to talk to me about cooking. As a result of this encounter, I've gotten into the habit of asking for His help when I go to the grocery store because I now know He's into the little things of my life like cooking. I want to talk to God so much that I hear Him on even the mundane things in life. If we are not careful, we will make God more spiritual than He really is and not realize that the same God that walked with Adam in the cool of the day is the same God that likes to walk with us in the everydayness of our lives.

The thing I love about building deep friendship with God is that we are always learning what He is like. We can't get to the end of Him. Just when you think you are so close to Him and understand how He is wired, He goes and says something that jars you. I was jarred when I heard Him talk to me about cooking in heaven. He knows what makes me happy and He spoke into my heart that day. Biblically speaking, this kind of response from God makes perfect sense. In the gospel of Luke, there are three parables involving different people—a joyful woman, a joyful servant, and a joyful father. Do you see a pattern? We will enter into His presence with joy and lots of celebration. I have come to find the Father, Jesus, and Holy Spirit to be the three most joyful persons I have ever met. God's personality is full of absolute joy and celebration. The part of this that should make us nervous is the reality that so many of His children on the earth don't seem to carry a lot of joy.

I've done the religious, depressed, miserable thing and now a lot of people call me strange because I have a high value for joy and celebration. I have noticed over the last fifteen years of walking with the Holy Spirit that some people I am around seem to have a difficult time "respecting" my leadership because there seems to be a presupposition that in order to lead on a high level in His kingdom, we need to be very serious people. Lightheartedness, childlike simplicity, joy, and celebration seem to be associated more with kids than adult leaders. Maybe we have the whole thing wrong. The other day a friend of mine was over at our house eating breakfast with my family. I had an impression from God to serve my friend's food on our red celebration plate for birthdays. When I put the plate on the table, my friend said, "How did you know it was my birthday?" The truth is that I did not know it was his birthday, but God did, and this small gesture from God through me touched his heart. Perhaps God is more lighthearted than we think. Perhaps He highly values celebration. Perhaps many of us are more serious than God is. Perhaps we have a distorted view of what seriousness should look like in the Kingdom of God.

I was praying over someone recently and God gave me a date. It happened to be this person's birthday. In moments like this, people are literally blown away that God cares about the whole world and also us as individuals. I have seen it happen time and time again—when I am giving words of knowledge over people and they break in an instant with joyful tears at the realization that the God who created all things loves to celebrate with us and the journey we are on with Him. So many of His kids fail to see that He sees us as clean as Jesus, and relates to us with a critical eye but not a critical spirit. I think we need to be really careful who we allow to speak into our lives on a continual basis. For example, why would I allow someone who has no fruit or joy in their life to teach me the ways of the Kingdom of God? We tend to value the intellect or influence of very serious people, and gravitate towards them, while ignoring the fact that there is very little if any proof of the fruit of joy and celebration in their lives. One of the things that I look for in people as evidence of the fruit of friendship with God is how they celebrate. We should be very nervous to open ourselves up for someone to influence us that does not value what God values.

I think we tend to assume that someone who walks in joy and celebration is just wired a certain way in his or her personality. I believe it has more to do with simply being connected to God in a deep way. It is absolutely impossible to be great friends with God and not carry these attributes. My life changed when I realized how much Jesus walked in these attributes during His life on the earth. When God gave me revelation that Jesus put a face on the Father, I became so excited to know that God is a person of joy and celebration. I have never in my life understood how someone can be a disciple, be leading in the Kingdom, and not carry joy and celebration on an ongoing basis. In so many ways, Jesus completely offended the religious culture of His day with these two attributes. He openly displayed a passion for joy and celebration. It is incredible to realize that even His first miracle of turning water into wine is a picture of these two values.

The Pharisees had large portions of the Scriptures memorized and yet got offended with how joyful Jesus was. Such things were looked down upon. Yet, along came their covenant-cutting God and said, "My first miracle will be wine at a celebration wedding." His opening act of the miraculous in the New Testament was making wine manifest. It was a lot of wine and was found to be absolutely delicious. If we are not careful, we will not be too much different from the Pharisees while ignoring the fact that Jesus is the same yesterday today and forever. Celebration is not something that He used to value. It is part and parcel of who He actually is. He is the God of celebration.

BEWARE THE CRITICAL SPIRIT

Years ago I had the revelation that Satan realized early on that he could not defeat the church so he just joined it. An example of this is that Satan absolutely loves to find someone who walks in a high level of wisdom in God's Kingdom and tip the scales of that wisdom so that it becomes a critical spirit. My wife reminded me recently that there is nothing wrong with having a critical eye. Notice I said "eye" and not "spirit." It is when we develop a critical spirit that we are actually playing the role of judge in people's lives. We were never called to judge one another. I want my airline pilot to have a critical eye at all times. I want my surgeon to have a critical eye as he operates on my body while using the competency that he or she has garnered through hard work and practice. A critical eye is not a critical spirit. A critical spirit says, "I know better than you. I am better than you. I see things more clearly than you do, and when you begin to think like me, you will be correct." It's rare for someone to realize they are struggling with a critical spirit. People who are judging others actually think they are walking in wisdom. The enemy is crafty in his ability to convince people that they are wiser than others when what is really happening is that the line of wisdom has been crossed into the land of judgement and criticism. The Father has no value for the critical spirit in any way. It is actually a snare in His Kingdom that we pronounce judgements upon our self when we judge. (See Matthew 7:1-5) Many times in my own life the Father has shown me that what I think is wisdom is actually me judging someone. It has been my experience in the prophetic that a critical spirit is the number one reason why people have a hard time hearing God. A critical spirit will put out the fire of the Holy Spirit.

This topic is so important to me because God has shown me that there is a high level of 1 Corinthians 14:1 to "Follow the way of love and eagerly desire gifts of the Spirit, especially prophecy" available to me when I honestly ask Him to help me see people the way He sees them. You see, the critical spirit and pride are best friends. There is nothing more dangerous to someone interested in building deep friendship with God than pride. Walking in the Kingdom with a critical spirit is literally like saying, "God, I do not want to connect with you or ever grow in the prophetic."

I'm not so sure we fully understand what is at stake when we develop a trait that opposes how God is wired. I believe with all of my heart that the Fear of the Lord is the beginning of all wisdom. (See Proverbs 9:10) When God showed me the consequences of having a critical spirit, it got my attention. Recently I was around some well-known ministers who have global ministries. God said to me as I was driving down to minister with them, "Chad, a ten percent critical spirit is 100 percent to me." It stopped me in my tracks. I said, "Holy Spirit, search me and know my heart and please show me anything that I need to confess." Over the next two hours, He began to show me that I have a loving heart but there was someone that I had developed a critical spirit toward and I needed to take that to the cross. To say this was a blind spot is an understatement. I thought that I was being wise and walking in truth with how I saw this person when instead, I had a problem on my hands because this is not at all how the Father saw them. I felt so clean after getting this off of my chest. The funny thing is, now this person is someone I talk to often and value at a much higher level.

Not too long ago, a close friend of mine came to me and told me that someone that I used to do life with was slandering me and saying things about me that were not true regarding my leadership and some decisions I had made concerning Bridgeway Church. As my friend shared details of what this particular person had been speaking against me, I discerned in my heart that the reason that I was finding out about this was that it was simply a test for me from the Father. I was tempted to defend myself and to do some self-loathing. Even though it has been three years since I have seen this person, I was tempted to be critical and bitter. When my friend left the room, I asked the Father to help me love unconditionally. Mind you, I had not seen this person for three years, and suddenly I just happened to bump into this person twice in the next week. We had a warm exchange and I was convinced beyond a shadow of a doubt that God was up to something. I am absolutely sure that our ability to forgive, love, and rid ourselves of any and all critical spirit towards another person is a sure way into the deepest place of the Father's heart.

Let's be honest, we've all been hurt, and most of us develop critical and judgmental thoughts toward those who have hurt us. We call it wisdom when what we are really saying is that we are better than they are. Satan is the master of trickery and, when we take the bait, He creates a paradigm in our minds that ties wisdom to a critical heart. When we ask the Father to literally give us the ability to see others the way He does, we are usually greatly surprised at how He has a critical eye but not a critical spirit. There is a reason why Paul says in 1 Corinthians 14:1 that we are to pursue love and then the gift of prophecy. Galatians 5:6 says that faith works by love. If you want to explode in your ability to connect with God and operate in the gifts of the Spirit, you simply need to ask the Father to do whatever it takes to remove all trace of a critical spirit in your heart and mind. The truth is that I put Jesus Christ on the cross. I actually deserve the deepest part of hell itself. It is only by His grace and love for me that I even have the opportunity to walk with God in the first place. We very rarely see this truth as a connection to operating in the prophetic, or even signs and wonders. The truth is that the recipe for explosive growth in our ability to deeply connect with God comes to us when we realize that we are called to simply love people while not considering ourselves better than anyone else. This is a perfect example of the opposite of carrying a critical spirit. This ancient principle that Paul shares is perhaps the gateway to a new level of not only walking with God, but seeing a high level of accuracy of hearing from Him ourselves.

LIVING AS GOD'S ORIGINAL

God loves an original. The more we get connected to Him, the more free we are to simply be ourselves and enjoy Him and the fact that He made us and is very comfortable with us being an original. I took my kids to the zoo recently and this point was made clear when I was standing there staring at the baboons. I'm not sure there is a more awkward looking animal in the world. The whole time I'm standing there looking at their flared red back side, I'm thinking, "Father, you made them." I'm sure at one point there was a thought of, "How about we put a monkey on the earth that looks awkward. How about we flare the butt and make it red just to keep things original and fun." Whether we like it or not, God has a sense of humor. Perhaps we get our humor from the Father Himself, since we are made in His image and likeness. As I stood there at the zoo that day I was keenly aware that the Father loves originals. I literally can't imagine what it must have been like for Noah to watch all of those animals board that boat. There were so many types of animals that God created. There are so many types of plants, trees, and flowers that came from the creative heart of God. Yet so many people who struggle to stay at the King's Table of intimacy with God find it almost impossible to believe that we are all original in God's eyes.

Recently I was ministering at a friend's church when the Father showed me a picture of how He values Kentucky Fried Chicken over Bojangles'. Now, I totally get that some people reading this will not take me seriously because God would "never say anything like this." Well, He showed me a picture indicating that He values the original over a copycat every single time. Why would He use Kentucky Fried Chicken? Because KFC prides itself for being the original fried chicken fast food restaurant. There have been many to emulate them over the years, like Bojangles', but the one thing that KFC can say is that they were the original fast food restaurant to sell fried chicken. God doesn't intend that we live as spiritual orphans, finding our identity in someone other than God Himself. We are each an original and He wants us to live like we know it.

The journey to our identity looks different for each of us. It is largely up to us. We start by getting into a place where we are not placing blame on anyone or anything for our lack of relationship with God. There needs to come a point where we simply say, "I can't live in Lo-debar anymore. I must pick up my mat and walk toward friendship with Him." We need to consecrate ourselves to God. The Hebrew word for consecration is Kadesh, which sounds a bit like something you put on a high-end taco in Manhattan. It means "consecrate, set apart, dedicate." Kadesh assumes personal responsibility and is driven by hunger. Hunger is about consecration. It is personal. No one can eat for me. Imagine going to a feast and saying, "No thank you, I will just be satisfied watching everyone else enjoy their food." Consecration is more than just looking religious, it is a personal decision to go through the season of pruning, discipline and sacrifice. It is laying down your own agenda for His. One of our greatest challenges is to get our identity from Elohim Himself. Father, Son, and Holy Spirit is where we find our greatest nourishment. When you get to the point of understanding your identity, and accepting the uniqueness of how He created you, and stop comparing yourself to others, you realize that you have reached a whole new level of consecration.

A LIGHT HEART

One of the secrets of building deep friendship with God is the ability to have a light heart. If we always associate heaviness with God, we'll miss Him 99 times out of 98. I love humor, laughter, and joy on a consistent basis. I am not talking about some sort of slapstick humor that is juvenile or silly. I'm simply talking about finding the humor in everyday life. Over the years, God has shown me that my ability to operate in the prophetic is directly related to the humor that He has helped me develop. His yoke is easy and His burden is light. There is a direct correlation between having a light heart and having the ability to hear him. Just the other night, I was laughing with some friends and a moment later I got into an Uber and had a prophetic word for our driver. I didn't have to go into some serious religious mode to do it. At God's core there is joy. He carries joy in the midst of seeing all the calamity in the world. If joy never leaves Him, it should never leave us. Please understand I am not associating joy with being irreverent or with weird humor. When I get calls from people in our church dealing with very heavy problems, I don't approach them with laughter. The Bible tells us clearly to mourn with those who mourn and rejoice with those who rejoice. (See Romans 12:15) I'm simply suggesting that there is a direct correlation with the ability to live with a light heart and have a deep friendship with God.

In Matthew 11:30 the Lord said that His yoke is easy and His burden is light. If the Lord's yoke is easy and His burden is light, then when I'm around you, I should feel lighter and more refreshed. So many Christ followers that I grew up with made me feel heavy and burdened. Because of this I literally associated God with a dreadful and heavy burden. I am convinced that a heavy, burdened heart is a roadblock to building deep friendship with God. For so long, I thought God hated me and that He killed my granddad. I thought He was the reason for my depression and anxiety. I had to allow God to rewire my brain because my thought patterns were so confused. Jesus loved to step into chaos and bring shalom and peace. The question that I want to be asking myself on a regular basis is, "Do I step into chaos and bring peace or is it the opposite?"

One of the fun realities of walking in deep friendship with God is that we begin to display His personality through our personality. I want people to think of me as someone who carries love, joy, peace, patience, kindness, goodness, faithfulness, gentleness, and self-control. Instead of beating ourselves up for what we lack in these areas, we need to simply ask Holy

Spirit to show us how to make the journey from Lo-debar to the King's Table, to that place where we can enjoy intimacy with the Father, Jesus, and Holy Spirit, and share in their characteristics. We should constantly be asking ourselves if we are moving towards the King's Table and who are we bringing with us.

Chapter 14

ASCEND

I **DECIDED TO TAKE MY OLDEST SON** on a retreat so we could talk about the birds and the bees. I love awkward moments, and you can usually find me cutting up about something with the Bridgeway family. I get really nervous around people who are always hyper-serious when it comes to conversations on the Kingdom and God. But as laid back as I am, I have to admit that I was more nervous than a wet black cat under a ladder about the awkward conversations that were to come as my 12-year-old Sam and I pulled away in the car. Even at 12, Sam was one of the most responsible teenagers I'd ever met. When other people ask Wendy and me, "How did you raise him? He's so mature." I respond, "We didn't. He raised us." Sam is one of the best friends that I have. It's been a fun experience for me to build a friendship with Sam that goes beyond simply being his father. The conversation in the car went something like this: "Sam, you and I are going to Athens, Georgia, to watch our Bulldogs play football, and we are going to make a weekend out of it. On Friday and Sunday, we are going to talk about sex for 15 total hours. We're going to go through Dennis Rainey's curriculum." Sam said, "OK."

On our way out of town, I stopped by the drugstore to buy some Nicorette gum to knock the edge off, and I don't even smoke. I needed something to get me to neutral. I had listened to a couple of the teachings in the curriculum ahead of time, but I was totally at a loss for words. There comes a time in a man's life when you encounter a brick wall so high that you can't help but be intimidated. I had learned about the birds and bees on the playground of Dawkins Middle School. Sam was about to learn about the whole shooting match from a 43-year-old man shaking in his boots. I never flinch speaking in front of big crowds of people, but I was more nervous about this than I would be walking naked through a crowded library.

The Dennis Rainey curriculum is a very well done resource that lets you listen to the teaching on CD and then process some reflective questions with your child. I put the first CD in as we headed to Athens. Thank God the first CD was tame. We digested it, and it did not cause too much awkward tension between Sammy and me. Our drive was only 90 minutes to the hotel, and that was the perfect amount of time to wrap up the first session. The weekend was off to a good start.

As the first session ended, I heard God say to me as clear as a bell, "Take Sam to see the movie *Everest* tonight in IMAX." Sometimes you wonder if it's God's voice or your own, but sometimes you know that it is 100 percent God. This was the latter. I guess God likes IMAX. I got on my iPhone and found out that *Everest* was playing 25 minutes from our hotel in an IMAX theatre. I was relieved to get away from the curriculum for the night. I had no idea that God would speak to me so powerfully through the movie that I would cry off and on throughout the entire movie.

Everest is about an expedition that attempted to climb to the summit of the most dangerous mountain in the world. The movie is based on the real-life story of a group of people who found out how deadly climbing Everest can be. Watching this movie on the IMAX screen left me with my mouth open and heart racing. Sam wondered why I was so emotional during the movie. It moved me on an emotional level that I don't go to often. In the middle of the movie, I had a prophetic download from heaven that flowed so long and hard that the best thing I can do is to share the whole thing in the paragraphs that follow. What I am about to write may not read like good writing, but I want to write it as I heard it. I pray that in some small way, it blesses you. A weekend that I thought was just about a time of bonding between my son and me on the topic of sexual purity turned out to be so much more.

Everest has a scene where the group arrives at basecamp and prepares to start their ascent up the mountain. That's when this prophetic download happened. It was like I went into a trance. I was watching the movie but also hearing from God and seeing images He was showing me that were on a level that I had not been accustomed to. I heard it like this:

> *Chad, everything is about to change for you. I am giving you an invitation to join Me on an adventure that will cost you greatly. I have been preparing you your entire life for what is now knocking on your door. Chad, there are places in Me that only a few go. Most people believe that the passage about walking the narrow road to find life in Me deals with going to heaven. The road to the top of Everest is a hard and thin road that only a few find. This road requires a death to self that many choose not*

to accept.

Two words are the major guides on this road, and those two words are "intimacy" and "obedience." With those two things, Chad, there is one other thing that will get you to the top of the mountain of God—perseverance. When you were young, you did what you wanted, but as you now begin the ascent up the mountain of God, you will lose all of your rights. You now have no more rights. When Jesus was in the Garden before offering His life on the cross, He relinquished everything to Me. The key to this journey is you staying in a place where all that you have is Mine. I want all of your heart.

As your Father, I know what is best for you, and I know what I want to do with you. The clarity of your destiny does not matter. The only thing that matters is that I have all of your heart. As you accept this invitation and leave base camp, I simply want you to give Me everything you have. This is why Jesus had His disciples travel lightly. There is such power when all you have is Me. Empty your pockets; empty your plans. People worry so much about making plans to change the world and then use My name as though I am a part of those plans. The only plan you need to focus on, Chad, is pursuing Me with your entire heart. Complete abandonment will get you going on your way to the top of this mountain.

Climbing the upcoming mountain will not be easy. The hordes of hell itself do not like it at all when one of My children decides he or she wants to leave base camp and climb to the top. I have tested you many times in your life. I am now extending you the invitation to start climbing a mountain you have never climbed. You have been so faithful to study and examine what this mountain is and what it costs. You have read so many books on men and women who have climbed this mountain of God. This mountain is Me. You have come to the end of yourself, and you truly desire to know Me and walk with Me without thoughts of your destiny or what I want to do with you.

Son, so many people come to Me in purity, but then quickly turn away from Me to pursue what is in life for themselves. Only a Luke 9:23 death and denial of self allows one to begin the ascent up this mountain. Selflessness is the key to great discoveries in Me. My people misunderstand Me often. I am not impressed with outward appearance or great exploits in My name as much as people think. I value the things that Jesus showed the world. We highly value selflessness. It's the core of what love is. The only people who are allowed to climb the mountain of God are people who want to discover Me for who I am and not for any glimpse of self-promotion or ambition. Many are invited to climb, but few know what it takes to get to the top.

Chad, the top of the mountain is a place where the air is thin and the only way for survival is intimacy with Me. I am so misunderstood. This is not about Me improving you. Chad, I am giving you an invitation to climb the mountain of God. I am inviting you to climb Me, and as you make your ascent, I am going to show you how to reside at the summit.

People have groomed themselves to think that you can't stay at my summit long. It's not true, Chad. When Jesus was on the earth, He grew in wisdom and in stature, and I groomed Him and grew Him to the place where He lived His entire life from my summit. Chad, it's possible to get so high in your thinking and experience with Me that you live above clouds that seem so dark to other people. You think you understand intimacy with Me. You have not even begun to enjoy Me yet. I want to show you things about Me that will blow your mind. I am going to show you how to climb this mountain. I am going to show you how to live as a dead person where no man can offend you. I am going to train you how to love well, to honor well, to forgive well, to get away from the things that snare so many of My children. This invitation, son, is an invitation to climb and reside.

Remember when you read Brother Lawrence's book? Do you remember how you told Me that you wanted to literally walk with Me every single day and never leave a conversation? Chad, it's possible. I'm not mad at you, and I have not been disappointed in you. One of the things that you struggle with is that you do not fully understand seed time and harvest. I'm not like you Americans. I take my time, and I value going slow. You have walked strong with me for years now, but it has taken some time for you to mature to the place where you can climb to the top of the mountain. The art of dying is one that is painful and many turn away from. I highly value complete abandonment.

Remember when Jesus told Peter after the resurrection, "When you were younger you dressed yourself and went where you wanted; but when you are old you will stretch out your hands, and someone else will dress you and lead you where you do not want to go" (John 21:18). Peter went through a transformation like so many others have with Me. There comes a point, Chad, where you reach the end of yourself and give Me something to work with. Jesus was completely sold out to Me, His Father. His death and resurrection is an invitation to the same type of life He lived.

We are continually amazed at how many people think of heaven as the goal. Chad, I am the goal. Relationship with Me is the goal. So many people who believe in Me and in heaven, and who have trusted in the cross have never let the DNA of the Gospel transform them from the inside out. I have so many children that believe in Me and know that they are coming to heaven, but they live so carnally and act more like the devil than they do my Son. Chad, I want you to reside on my summit and invite others to take the journey to join you. That's what this is about Chad. I'm not calling you to invite people to heaven as a place. I'm calling you to lead people to Me, your Abba.

Chad, I am tender. I am so tender. It is My pure pleasure to reveal Myself to My true friends. I love so deeply, but I do not trust everyone. People confuse My love with My trust. I elevate those in my Kingdom whom I trust. Climbing to the summit is about deep friendship and trust. I enjoy watching people discover what I had with Moses on the earth. People find it so odd that I was so close to Moses. Son, I enjoy friendship more than you do. I invented friendship. It is written, "Let us make man in our image" (Genesis 1:26). We are community. We are friendship. The journey to the summit is not a climb to please God. The journey to the summit is to become dear friends with Us. I did not send Jesus to the cross to get you to heaven when you die. I sent Jesus to the cross to provide an opportunity to reenter the garden of deep friendship and intimacy with Us. We love people deeply.

Chad, I want you to experience deep things with Me, your Father, on the summit, and then help people understand what is available to them. So many of My followers have built their ministries upon getting people to heaven. Son, your ministry will be built on getting people to Me. My call on your life is for you to help people come through the blood of Jesus to Me. I have not changed. My personality is not changing. I've always valued intimacy. It's who I am. It's who We are.

Come to me Chad. Climb this mountain. We've known each other a long, long time, but I am about to show you that there is so much more. Don't ever pursue a stage. Don't network yourself and do what so many others do. You do not need a resume, credentials, or the connections with other people to get you where you need to be. You need Me, son. I am with you. I am with you. Son, I am with you. Climb.

With my son sitting to my right, I typed those words on my phone. I'm not actually sure what this experience was. Was it a trance? I don't know. I can say that it was as though God sat down right beside me and talked to me tenderly. I know when God is near because I cry a lot. I realize He lives inside me, but sometimes His presence draws so close that it's as though there is a thin veil between me and the realm of heaven. I'm sure you know what I mean. In that moment, I was reminded for the millionth time in my walk with God how much He truly values relationship.

WHAT WE CAN LEARN

As I close this book, I want to attempt to break down my prophetic download from God to help us discern practically what it means to leave base camp and start the ascent up His mountain.

1. Being prophetic and walking in power is not a charismatic idea. It stems from intimacy.

Many people who love Jesus with their whole hearts still choose to keep this conversation about the supernatural in the "weird" category because they think that it is only for charismatics. The more I pay attention to Jesus in the gospels, the more that I notice that He never went around trying to make people charismatic. He simply built deep intimacy with His heavenly Father, did what His Father wanted Him to do, and said what His Father wanted Him to say. He even called the supernatural stuff the Father's works. (See John 10:38)

Perhaps we do not see the same works of the Father because we do not know the Father the way Jesus did. The enemy tricks us into thinking that supernatural ministry has to be weird. Just because someone on late-night television portrays healing and deliverance as weird, it does not mean that their opinion is true or even biblical. What we've talked about in this book is an intimacy conversation more than it is a charismatic conversation.

2. Supernatural ministry is lived from the summit. The power to do extraordinary things with God comes from the oil of friendship with Him.

Before Jesus picked His 12 disciples, He spent all night praying. We tend to assume that Jesus operated in power strictly from His anointing. As we evaluate His life closely, it is easy to see that much of what He accomplished came from growing in favor and wisdom with God the Father. (See Luke 2:52) Climbing to the summit is not just for warm feelings of friendship with God. The goal is actually to transform us into the very image of His son Jesus, and to get us into position to destroy the works of the enemy.

3. The pathway to the summit is Luke 9:23—Death to self.

I used to think that Jesus Christ came to be the way to heaven. Over the last 15 years, I have come to realize that Jesus also came to show us a picture of what our lives can be like. I don't see people healed when I pray for them because I read some charismatic book that told me I can. I actually read the gospel of John over 500 times and noticed that Jesus kept showing His disciples that they could do the same works He was doing. He kept showing them that deep friendship with God produced power inside that has the ability to step into brokenness and bring wholeness. The closer Jesus got to the cross, the more He continued to lay His life down in utter dependence on the Father. His life was an offering laid out before God. His invitation is for us to do the same. The lower I get before the Father, the more He elevates me in a position to walk a powerful life that helps others.

4. The summit is not heaven itself. Rather, it is the Father.

For many years, people have been led to the Lord with this question: "If you died right now, do you know where you would go?" There is nothing inherently evil in this question. Yet, I have deep concern over this thought process because we do not see Jesus operating this way when He was in ministry. Jesus was and is constantly being the bridge to the Father, not to a place called heaven. Heaven is great and will be wonderful one day, but the reason it will be wonderful is because the Father is there. I sometimes wonder if many evangelicals would care if the Father was even there or not when they arrive.

We have spent so much time thinking through the place to avoid and the place to go that I believe we miss the whole point of the cross in the first place. The Gospel is the good news that I get to be reconnected to the Father through the blood of Jesus Christ once I put my faith in the person of Jesus. This is what the summit is all about. I tell people often, "When you walk in a high level of revelation of who you are in Christ, you will see more people healed on accident than you would on purpose any other way." We simply learn to give away what we have when we abide on the summit.

5. Higher thinking is the slingshot up the mountain.

Colossians 3:1-3 sums it up best as Paul says, "Set your hearts and minds on things above . . ." I used to think that it was a little condemning when God said that His thoughts were higher than our thoughts. I don't think that anymore. I believe that the Father is simply saying, "Chad, come on up here. I'll train you how to view every situation through My lens, son. I'll train you the same way that I trained Jesus. You will grow in My favor and wisdom if you will simply get higher."

At Bridgeway, you will often hear someone say from stage, "We need to get higher." In order to climb the mountain of God, we must get higher in our thinking. I grew up in a church where a man used to say, "Don't be so heavenly minded that you can't live down here on earth." Now, I actually like the opposite of that thought: "Don't be so earthly minded that you don't allow heaven to be unleashed through you."

The Father loves it when His children move out of base camp and start ascending the mountain of intimacy through the transformation of the mind. There is a reason that Paul wrote 189 times in his letters "in Christ" or "in him." Paul was desperately trying to help the saints understand the exchange that happened at the cross. Calvary was and is an invitation into an exchange. We are not weak, helpless, frail, dirty, or lost. We are as clean as Jesus and no longer filthy in His presence. (See Colossians 1:21-22) Higher thinking slings us up the mountain.

MAMA JANE

I love when Hebrews 12:1 says that we are surrounded by such a great cloud of witnesses. Have you ever considered that this idea may be more literal than we think? I know that God is with us, as I can theologically prove that to be accurate. I also wonder if there are times when the Father allows our loved ones, who have gone before us and who are now in heaven, to know what we are putting our hands to. I guess we will find out one day for sure. In the meantime, I have often pondered if that Hebrews passage is more literal than we think. Perhaps all of heaven is cheering us on as we build deep friendship with God and extend His Kingdom on the earth.

My hero is Jane Norris, who has been in heaven with Jesus for a few years now. Mama Jane was my grandmother, mentor, friend, and prayer partner; but most importantly, she was my hero. The Father has given me some tremendous gifts in my life. I could not have found a better woman to share my life with and raise children with other than Wendy. I could have searched the earth and not have found a better spouse. My three kids all amaze me, and it is purely a blessing that God gave them to me. I have parents who have always loved me and never gave up on me, siblings whom I adore, and friends who are some of the best people on this planet. God has been so good to me, and yet when I think about the woman who had such a large impact on my life, and who is now in heaven, I want to say to God, "You were too good to me." Some blessings overwhelm you to the place where you feel so unworthy. That's who Jane was and is to me. It's going to be a little awkward to meet her again in her newly renovated self. I've always known her as my older grandmother. I'm sure that day will be strange for all of us.

Recently, not long after my encounter during the Everest movie, I had the most intense dream I've ever had in all my years on this earth. It was so intense that I felt like I was in another realm. My body was even a bit sore when I woke up the next morning. In the dream, I was standing inside a majestic looking room with my grandmother. She was around 30 years old with jet-black hair. The room had these gorgeous flowers that I had never seen before. All the walls were actually windows overlooking mountains so astounding and beautiful that I can't even begin to describe it. The view took my breath away. I looked around the room and remember thinking in the dream, "This place is unreal." I knew that I was dreaming. It's odd to me to even think about how these things work. My grandmother never looked up at me, but she kept looking at the very large book she was reading. The book was called *The Oracles of God*. She knew I was in the room. She sat there for what seemed like 10 minutes before she spoke. I was not about to say a word because there was a part of me that was scared to be there. In my dream, I knew this was legit. As I was looking at Jane, she said softly in the exact same voice I still remember, "Sweetie, it's time to ascend the mountain of God." I could not tell exactly, but I believe she was reading from Ezekiel.

As soon as Mama Jane said this, I walked outside with my dad in the dream. My dad and I were playing golf just outside of Mama Jane's house. All of a sudden, my dad fell down and had a heart attack. He died right in front of me. I picked him up with my left hand, blew on his face, and he came back to life. After he came back to life, we walked back through Mama Jane's house to literally the most beautiful scene I have ever seen in my life. I know it was just a dream, but it was so real. It was in the evening, and there was the most beautiful snowfall I've ever seen. The snowflakes were huge, and a white feather gently circled each one. I looked at my dad with this enormous mountain in the background and said, "I love it when the angels show up." When I said that, I woke up so dramatically in my bed that I gasped for air. My body felt like it weighed 500 pounds, and it wasn't from the pasta I ate the night before. I woke my wife up and said, "Babe, you are not going to believe this."

The dream with my grandmother telling me to ascend the mountain of God coming on the heels of God putting me in a trance during the movie *Everest* was soon followed by the strangest thing God has ever asked me to do. It was only three months after this that God told me to fly to Azusa Street, lick the ground, and fly back to Bridgeway Church and spit on the ground. He had prepared me. Even though I did not understand the act itself, I knew that ascending the mountain means radical obedience without the right to explanations.

BENEDICTION

More than anything, I desire to see God move all over the world in power. I want Him to start with me. It has to be possible to see naturally supernatural cultures established everywhere by His sons and daughters who are abiding and feasting at the King's Table. It happened in the Book of Acts. It's been happening since then in pockets of places where people experience the things that the Father is so passionate about. He still loves to heal and deliver. He still loves to use common people to do extraordinary things in His Kingdom. He still desires family and deep friendship with His sons and daughters.

I sincerely pray that you will take a step out of the boat toward the invitation to walk away from spiritual orphanhood in Lo-debar and take your seat at the King's Table as a spiritual son or daughter. I pray you will also accept the invitation to live a supernatural life—a life where your common church starts seeing uncommon breakthrough because you are willing to lead in courageous ways. I pray that you decide to become passionate about the things that Jesus was so passionate about in His ministry. Other people's breakthrough hinges on our desire to be courageous and lead out in the way Jesus would lead out if He were on the earth leading our churches. He was passionate about God's family then and He is now. He was passionate about re-connecting us to Eden, about inviting us to the King's Table then, and He is now. He was passionate about the supernatural then, and He is now.

Come, Lord Jesus. Help us.

"I give all my praises and glory to the one who has more than enough power to make you strong and keep you steadfast though the promises found in the wonderful news that I preach; that is, the proclamation of Jesus, the Anointed One. This wonderful news includes the unveiling of the mystery kept secret from the dawn of creation until now. This mystery is understood through the prophecies of the Scripture and by the decree of the eternal God. And it is now heard openly by all the nations, igniting within them a deep commitment of faith. Now to God, the only source of wisdom, be glorious praises for the endless ages through Jesus, the Anointed One! Amen!" (Romans 16:25-27 TPT).

Please allow me to leave you with a blessing.

May you take John 14:12 seriously.
May you not take yourself too seriously.
May you build deep friendship with the Father.
May you release His love to others
and smile as the works of the enemy are
destroyed in their lives.
May you accept your own heavenly acceptance.
He loved you enough to die for you. He does not merely
tolerate you. He loves you.
May His kindness lead you to repentance
till your last breath.

God is calling you into the greatest friendship the world has ever known.

For additional resources, teaching, and content, please visit

MamaJanesSecret.com

dive deeper into identity, family, living a naturally supernatural lifestyle, being seated at the king's table, and more

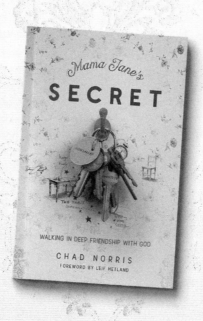

Chad Norris is the Lead Pastor of Bridgeway Church in Greenville, SC. He has traveled for years sharing a message of Father's love and the simple truth that we have the ability to build deep friendship with God. Chad's passion is to know Father and to introduce others to the concept that He is kind and good and desires to be connected to His kids. Father wants His family back. Chad brings a humor  and vulnerability to messages that reflect his own intimacy with Father and his love of the Word. Bridgeway Church is a family that honors the Word of God and the power of Holy Spirit.

Chad and his wife, Wendy are Bulldogs, both graduates of the University of Georgia. He has a Masters of Divinity from Beeson Divinity School and is working toward a Doctorate at Regent University. The Norris family are passionate to create a culture of discipleship that begins in their own home and extends to everything they do.